PREFACE.

The masters of music, Haydn, Mozart and Bee
beyond the limits of their predecessors by ide   ___ more
closely with the development of active life itself. By their creative power
they invested the life of the nation and mankind with profounder thought,
culminating at last in the most sublime of our possessions—religion. No
artist has followed in their course with more determined energy than
Richard Wagner, as well he might, for with equal intellectual capacity, the
foundation of his education was broader and deeper than that of the classic
masters; while on the other hand the development of our national character
during his long active career, became more vigorous and diversified as the
ideas of the poets and thinkers were more and more realized and reflected
in our life. Wagner's development was as harmonious as that of the three
classic masters, and all his struggles, however violent at times, only cleared
his way to that high goal where we stand with him to-day and behold the
free unfolding of all our powers. This goal is the entire combination of all
the phases of art into one great work: the music-drama, in which is
mirrored every form of human existence up to the highest ideal life. As this
music-drama rests historically upon the opera it is but natural that the
second triumvirate of German music should be composed of the founder
of German opera, C. M. von Weber, the reformer of the old opera,
Christoph Wilibald Gluck, and Richard Wagner. To trace therefore the
development of the youngest of these masters, will lead us to consider
theirs as well, and in doing this the knowledge of what he is will disclose
itself to us.

CHAPTER I.

1813-1831.

WAGNER'S EARLY YOUTH.

His Birth—The Father's Death—His Mother Remarries—Removal to Dresden—Theatre and Music—At School—Translation of Homer—Through Poetry to Music—Returning to Leipzig—Beethoven's Symphonies—Resolution to be a Musician—Conceals this Resolution—Composes Music and Poetry—His Family Distrusts his Talent—"Romantic" Influences—Studies of Thoroughbass—Overture in B major—Theodor Weinlig—Full Understanding of Mozart—Beethoven's Influence—The Genius of German Art—Preparatory Studies ended.

"I resolved to be a musician."—Wagner.

Richard Wilhelm Wagner was born in Leipzig, May 22, 1813. His father at that time was superintendent of police—a post which, owing to the constant movement of troops during the French war, was one of special importance. He soon fell a victim to an epidemic which broke out among the troops passing through. The mother, a woman of a very refined and spiritual nature, then married the highly gifted actor, Ludwig Geyer, who had been an intimate friend of the family, and removed with him to Dresden, where he held a position at the court theatre and was highly esteemed. There Wagner spent his childhood and early youth. Besides the great patriotic uprising of the German people, artistic impressions were the first to stir his soul. His father had taken an active interest in the amateur theatricals of the Leipzig of his day, and now the family virtually identified themselves with the practical side of the art. His brother Albert and sister Rosalie subsequently joined the theatre, and two other sisters diligently devoted themselves to the piano. Richard himself satisfied his childish tendency by playing comedy in his own room and his piano-playing was confined to the repetition of melodies which he had heard. His step-father, during the sickness which also overtook him, heard Richard play two melodies, the "Ueb' immer Treu und Redlichkeit" and the "Jungfernkranz" from "Der Freischuetz," which was just becoming known at that time. The boy heard him say to his mother in an undertone: "Can it be that he has a talent for music?" He had destined him to be an artist, being himself as good a portrait painter as he was actor. He died, however, before the boy had reached his seventh year, bequeathing to him only the information imparted to his mother, that he "would have made something out of him." Wagner in the first sketch of his life, (1842) relates that for a long time he

Life of Wagner

Ludwig Nohl

Alpha Editions

This edition published in 2022

ISBN : 9789356899377

Design and Setting By
Alpha Editions
www.alphaedis.com
Email - info@alphaedis.com

Contents

dwelt upon this utterance of his step-father; and that it impelled him to aspire to greatness.

His inclinations however did not at first turn to music. He was rather disposed to study and was sent to the celebrated Kreuzschule. Music was only cultivated indifferently. A private teacher was engaged to give him piano lessons, but, as in drawing, he was averse to the technicalities of the art, and preferred to play by ear, and in this way mastered the overture to "Der Freischuetz." His teacher upon hearing this expressed the opinion that nothing would become of him. It is true, he could not in this way acquire fingering and scales, but he gained a peculiar intonation arising from his own deep feeling, that has been rarely possessed by any other artist. He was very partial to the overture to "The Magic Flute," but "Don Juan" made no impression on him.

All this, however, was only of secondary importance. The study of Greek, Latin, mythology, and ancient history so completely captivated the active mind of the boy, that his teacher advised him seriously to devote himself to philological studies. As he had played music by imitation so he now tried to imitate poetry. A poem, dedicated to a dead schoolmate, even won a prize, although considerable fustian had to be eliminated. His richness of imagination and feeling displayed itself in early youth. In his eleventh year he would be a poet! A Saxon poet, Apel, imitated the Greek tragedies, why should he not do the same? He had already translated the first twelve books of Homer's "Odyssey," and had made a metrical version of Romeo's monologue, after having, simply to understand Shakspeare, thoroughly acquired a knowledge of English. Thus at an early age he mastered the language which "thinks and meditates for us," and Shakspeare became his favorite model. A grand tragedy based on the themes of Hamlet and King Lear was immediately undertaken, and although in its progress he killed off forty-two of the *dramatis personae* and was compelled in the denouement, for want of characters to let their ghosts reappear, we can not but regard it as a proof of the superabundance of his inborn power.

One advantage was secured by this absurd attempt at poetry: it led him to music, and in its intense earnestness he first learned to appreciate the seriousness of art, which until then had appeared to him of such small importance in contrast with his other studies, that he regarded "Don Juan" for instance as silly, because of its Italian text and "painted acting," as disgusting. At this time he had grown familiar with "Der Freischuetz," and whenever he saw Weber pass his house, he looked up to him with reverential awe. The patriotic songs sung in those early days of resurrected Germany appealed to his sensitive nature. They fascinated him and filled his earnest soul with enthusiasm. "Grander than emperor or king, is it to stand there and rule!" he said to himself, as he saw Weber enchant and sway the souls of his auditors with his "Freischuetz" melodies. He now returned with the family to Leipzig. Did he, while at work on his grand tragedy, occupying him fully two years, neglect his studies? In the Nicolai school, where he now attended, he was put back one class, and this so disheartened him, that he lost all interest in his studies. Besides, now for the first time, the actual spirit of music illumined his intellectual horizon. In the Gewandhaus concerts he heard Beethoven's symphonies. "Their impression on me was very powerful," he says, speaking of his deep agitation, though only in his fifteenth year, and it was still further intensified when he was informed that the great master had died the year previous, in pitiful seclusion from all the world. "I knew not what I really was intended for," he puts in the mouth of a young musician in his story, "A Pilgrimage to Beethoven," written many years after. "I only remember, that I heard a symphony of Beethoven one evening. After that I fell sick with a fever, and when I recovered, I was a musician." He grew lazy and negligent in school, having only his tragedy at heart, but the music of Beethoven induced him to devote himself passionately to the art. Indeed while listening to the Egmont music, it so affected him that he would not for all the world, "launch" his tragedy without such music. He had perfect confidence that he could compose it, but nevertheless thought it advisable to acquaint himself with some of the rules of the art. To accomplish this at once, he borrowed for a week, an easy system of thoroughbass. The study did not seem to bear fruit as quickly as he had expected, but its difficulties allured his energetic and active mind. "I resolved to be a musician," he said. Two strong forces of modern society, general education and music, thus in early youth made an impression upon his nature. Music conquered, but in a form which includes the other, in the presentation of the poetic idea as it first found its full expression in Beethoven's symphonies. Let us now see how this somewhat arbitrary and selfwilled temperament urged the stormy young soul on to the real path of his development.

The family discovered his "grand tragedy." They were much grieved, for it disclosed the neglect of his school studies. Under the circumstances he concealed his consciousness of his inner call to music, secretly continuing, however, his efforts at composition. It is noticeable that the impulse to adapt poetry never forsook him, but it was made subordinate to the musical faculty. In fact the former was brought into requisition only to gratify the latter, so completely did musical composition control him. Beethoven's Pastoral symphony prompted him at one time to write a shepherd play, which owed its dramatic construction on the other hand to Goethe's vaudeville, "A Lover's Humor," to which he wrote the music and the verses at the same time, so that the action and movement of the play grew out of the making of the verses and the music. He was likewise prompted to compose in the prevailing forms of music, and produced a sonata, a string quartet, and an aria.

These works may not have had faults as far as form is concerned, but very likely they were without any intrinsic value. His mind was still engrossed with other things than the real poesy of music. Notwithstanding this, under cover of such performances as these, he believed he could announce himself to the family as a musician. They regarded such efforts at composition however as a mere transitory passion, which would disappear like others especially so as he was not proficient on even one instrument, and could not therefore assume to do the work of a practical musician with any degree of assurance. At this time a strange and confused impression was made upon the young mind, which had already absorbed so much of importance. The so called "romantic writers" who then reigned supreme, particularly the mystic Hoffmann, who was both poet and musician, and who wrote the most beautiful poetic arrangements of the works of Gluck, Mozart, and Beethoven, along with the absurdest notions of music, tended to completely disturb his poetic ideas and mode of expression in music. This youth of scarce sixteen was in danger of losing his wits. "I had visions both waking and sleeping, in which the key note, third and quint appeared bodily and demonstrated their importance to me, but whatever I wrote on the subject was full of nonsense," he says himself.

It was high time to overcome and settle these disturbing elements. His imperfect understanding of the science of music, which had given rise to these fancies and apparitions, now gave place to its real nature, its fixed rules and laws. The skilled musician, Mueller, who subsequently became organist at Altenburg, taught him to evolve from those strange forms of an overwrought imagination the simple musical intervals and accords, thus giving his ideas a secure foundation even in these musical inspirations and fantasies. Corresponding success however, had not yet been attained in the practical groundwork of the art. The impetuous young fellow and enthusiast continued inattentive and careless in this study. His intellectual nature was too restless and aggressive to be brought back easily to the study of dry technical rules, and yet its progress was not far-reaching enough, for even in art their acquisition is essential.

One of the grand overtures for orchestra which he chose to write at that time instead of giving himself to the study of music as an independent language, he called himself the "culmination of his absurdities." And yet in this composition, in B major, there was something, which, when it was performed at the Leipzig Gewandhaus, commanded the attention of so thorough a musician as Heinrich Dorn, then a friend of Wagner, and who became later Oberhofkapellmeister at Berlin. This was the poetic idea which Wagner by the aid of his mental culture was enabled to produce in music, and which gives to a composition its inner and organic completeness. Dorn could thus sincerely console the young author with the hope of future success for his composition, which, instead of a favorable reception, met only with indignation and derision.

The revolution which broke out in France in July, 1830, greatly excited him as it did others and he even contemplated writing a political overture. The fantastic ideas prevalent at that time among the students at the university, which in the meantime he had entered to complete his general education, and fit himself thoroughly for the vocation of a musician, tended still further to divert his mind from the serious task before him. At this juncture, both for his own welfare and that of art, a kind Providence sent him a man, who, sternly yet kindly, as the storm subsided, directed the awakening impulse for order and system in his musical studies. This was Theodore Weinlig, who had been cantor at the Thomasschule in Leipzig, since 1823 and was therefore, so to speak, bred in the spirit and genius of the great Sebastian Bach. He possessed that attribute of a good teacher which leads the scholar imperceptibly into the very heart of his study. In less than a year the young scholar had mastered the most difficult problems of counterpoint, and was dismissed by his teacher as perfectly competent in his art. How highly Wagner esteemed him is shown by the fact that his "Liebesmahl der Apostel," his only work in the nature of an oratorio, is dedicated to "Frau Charlotte Weinlig, the widow of my never-to-be-forgotten teacher." During this time he also composed a sonata and a polonaise, both of which were free from bombast and simple and natural in their musical form. More important than all, Wagner now began to understand Mozart and learned to admire him. He was at last on the path which subsequently was to lead him, even nearer than Beethoven came, to that mighty cantor of Leipzig, who by his art has disclosed for all time the depths of our inner life and sanctified them.

For the present it was Beethoven, whose art unfolded itself before him, and now that his own knowledge was firmly grounded, aided him to become a composer. "I doubt whether there has ever been a young musician more familiar with Beethoven's works than was Wagner, then eighteen years of age," says Dorn of this period. Wagner himself says in his "Deutscher Musiker in Paris:" "I knew no greater pleasure than that of throwing myself so completely into the depths of this genius that I imagined I had become a part of him." He copied the master's overtures and the Ninth symphony, the latter causing him to sob violently, but at the same time rousing his highest enthusiasm. He now also fully comprehended Mozart, especially his Jupiter symphony. "In the genius of our fatherland, pure in feeling and chaste in inspiration, he saw the sacred heritage wherewith the German, under any skies and whatever language he might speak, would be certain to preserve the innate grandeur of his race," is his opinion of Mozart expressed in Paris a few years afterward. "I strove for clearness and power," he says of this period of his youth, and an overture and a symphony soon demonstrated that he had really grasped the models. After twenty years of personal activity in this high school of art, he succeeded in thoroughly understanding the great Sebastian Bach, and reared on this solid foundation-stone of music the majestic edifice of German art, which embraces all the capabilities and ideals of the soul, and created at last a national drama, complete in every sense.

The school period was passed. He now entered active life with firm and secure step, armed only with his knowledge and his power of will. In his struggles and disappointments the former was to be put to the test and the latter to be strengthened. We shall meet with him again, when by the exercise of these two powers he has gained his first permanent victories.

CHAPTER II.

1832-1841.

STORM AND STRESS.

In Vienna—His Symphony Performed—Modern Ideas—"The Fairies,"—
"Das Liebesverbot"—Becomes Kapellmeister—Mina Planer—Hard
Times—Experiences and Studies—"Rienzi"—Paris—First
Disappointments—A Faust Overture—Revival of the German Genius—
Struggle for Existence—"The Flying Dutchman"—Historical Studies—
Returning to Germany.

The God who in my breast resides,
He cannot change external forces.—Goethe.

Beethoven's life has acquainted us with the pre-eminence of Vienna as a
musical centre. In the summer of 1832 Wagner visited the city, but found
himself greatly disappointed as he heard on all sides nothing but "Zampa,"
and the potpourris of Strauss. He was not to see the imperial city again
until late in life and as the master, crowned with fame. In music and the
opera Paris had the precedence. The Conservatory in Prague however
performed his symphony, though right here he was destined to feel that the
reign of his beloved Beethoven had but scarcely begun.

In the succeeding winter the same symphony was performed in Leipzig.
"There is a resistless and audacious energy in the thoughts, a stormy bold
progression, and yet withal a maidenly artlessness in the expression of the
main motives that lead me to hope for much from the composer;" so wrote
Laube, with whom Wagner had shortly before become acquainted. Here
again we recognize the stormy, restless activity of the time, which
thenceforth did not cease, and brought about the unity of the nation and of
art. The ideas which prevailed among the students' clubs, the theories of St.
Simon and would-be reformers generally had captivated the young artist's
mind. In the "Young Europe," Laube advocated the liberal thoughts of the
new century, the intoxication of love, and all the pleasures of material life.
Wagner's head was full of them and Heine's writings and the sensual
"Ardinghello" of Heinse helped to intensify them.

For a time however his better nature retained the mastery. Beethoven and
Weber remained his good genii. In 1833 he composed an opera, "The
Fairies," modelled after their works, the text of which displayed the earnest
tendency of his nature. A fairy falls in love with a mortal but can acquire

human life only on condition that her lover shall not lose faith and desert her, however wicked and cruel she may appear. She transforms herself into a stone from which condition the yearning songs of her lover release her. It is a characteristic feature of Wagner's ideal conception of love that the lover then is admitted to the perpetual joys of the fairy world, as a reward for his faith in the object of his love. The work was never performed. Bellini, Adam, and their associates controlled the stage in Germany, and he was greatly disappointed. That grand artiste, Schroeder-Devrient, who afterwards was to become so essential to Wagner, had achieved unusual success in these light operas, especially in the role of *Romeo*. He observed this and comparing the sparkling music of these French and Italians with the German Kapellmeister-music which was then coming into vogue, it seemed indeed tedious and tormenting. Why should not he then, this youth of twenty-one, ready for any deed and every pleasure, earnestly longing for success, enter upon the same course? Beethoven appeared to him as the keystone of a great epoch to be followed by something new and different. The fruit of this restless seething struggle was "Das Liebesverbot oder die Novize von Palermo," his first opera which reached a performance.

The material was taken from Shakspeare's "Measure for Measure," not however without making its earnestness conform to the ideas of "Young Europe," and leaving the victory to sensualism. *Isabella*, the novice, begs of the puritanical governor her brother's life, who has forfeited it through some love affair. The governor agrees to grant the pardon, on condition that she shall yield to his desires. A carnival occurs, and, as in "Masaniello," a young man who loves the maiden, incites a revolution, exposes the governor, and receives *Isabella's* hand. The spirit which pervades this tempestuous carnival pleasure is sufficiently characterized by a verse in the only chorus-number, which has appeared in print from this opera: "Who does not rejoice in our pleasure plunge the knife into his breast!"

There were, it will be observed, two radically different possibilities of development. The "sacred fervor of his sensitive soul," which he had nourished with the German instrumental music, had encountered the tendency to sensualism, and, as we find so often in Wagner's works, these two elements of our nature were powerfully portrayed, with the victory ever remaining to the judicious and serious conception of life. Struggles and sorrows of various kinds were to bring this "sacred earnestness" again into the foreground, to remain there forever afterward.

In the autumn of 1834, during which this text had been written, Wagner accepted the position of Kapellmeister at the Magdeburg theatre and thus entered the field of practical activity. The position suited him and he soon proved himself an able director, especially for the stage. His skill in music, composed for the passing moment, soon gained for him the desired success and induced him to compose the music to the "Liebesverbot." "It often gave me a childish pleasure to rehearse these light, fashionable operas, and to stand at the director's desk and let the thing loose to the right and left," he tells us. He did not seek in the least to avoid the French style but on the contrary felt confident, that an actress like Schroeder-Devrient could even in such frivolous music invest his *Isabella* with dignity and value. With such expectations in art and life before him, he took unhesitatingly the serious step of engaging himself to Mina Planer, a beautiful actress at the Magdeburg theatre, who unfortunately however was never destined to appreciate his nobler aspirations.

In the spring of 1836, before the dissolution of the Magdeburg troupe, an overhasty presentation of his opera was given, the only one that ever took place. It was said of it by one: "There is much in it, and it is very pleasing. There is that music and melody, which we so rarely find in our distinctive German operas." He had himself for some time completely neglected "The Fairies." The score of both operas is in the possession of King Louis of Bavaria. They were to be followed by one destined to survive—"Rienzi."

He had sought in vain to secure a performance of the "Liebesverbot," first in Leipzig, then in Berlin. In the latter city he saw one of Spontini's operas performed and for the first time fully recognized the meagre resources of the native stage, particularly in scenic presentation. How Paris must have aroused his longing where Spontini had introduced the opera upon a grander scale and with stronger ensemble! The financial difficulties however, which followed the dissolution of the Magdeburg theatre and the failure of his compositions forced him to continue his connection still longer with the German stage, wretched as it was. He next went to Koenigsberg. The position there was not sufficiently remunerative to protect him from want, now that he was married. One purpose he kept constantly in view, namely, to perform some splendid work of art and with it free himself from his embarrassing position. In every interesting romance he sought the material for a grand opera. Among others, he selected Koenig's "Hohe Braut," rapidly arranged the scenes and sent the manuscript to Scribe in Paris, whose endorsement was considered essential, and whose "Huguenots" had just helped to make Meyerbeer one of the stars of the day. Nothing came of it however. Of what importance in this direction was Germany at that time? The Koenigsberg troupe was also soon dissolved. "Some men are at once decisive in their character and their works, while others have first to fight their way through a chaos of passions. It is true however that the latter class obtain greater results," it is said in one account of this short episode. He was soon to accomplish such an achievement. In the city of Koenigsberg, the old seat of the Prussian kings, he had won a friend for life who, as will subsequently appear, proved of service to him. The general character of life in Prussia also greatly contributed to strengthen in him that independent bearing of which Spontini's imperious splendor had given him a hint, and which subsequently was to invest his own art with so much importance in the world's history.

During a visit to Dresden in 1837 he came across Bulwer's "Rienzi, the Last of the Tribunes," in which he became deeply interested, the more so that the hero had been in his mind for some time. The necessities of subsistence now drove him across the borders to Riga. His Leipzig friend Dorn was there, and Karl Holtei had just organized a new theatre. He was made director of music and his wife appeared in the leading feminine roles. Splendid material was at hand and Wagner went zealously to work. He was obliged however to produce here also the works of Adam, Auber, and Bellini, which gave him a still deeper insight into the degradation of the modern stage, with its frivolous comedy, of which he had a perfect horror. About this time he became familiar with the legend of the "Flying Dutchman," as Heine relates it, with the new version that love can release the Ahasuerus of the sea. The "fabulous home sickness," of which Heine speaks, found an echo in his own soul and excited it the more. He studied moreover Mehul's "Joseph in Egypt" and under the influence of the grave and noble music of this imitator of the great Gluck, he felt himself "elevated and purified." Even Bellini's "Norma," under the influence of such impressions, gained a nobler tone and more dignified form than is really inherent in the music. "Norma" was at that time even given for his benefit! He now took up the "Rienzi" material in earnest and projected a plan for the work which required the largest stage for its execution. The lyric element of the romance, the messengers of peace, the battle hymns, and the passion of love had already charmed his purely musical sense. It was however by a solid work for the theatre, of which the main feature should not be simply "beautiful verses and fine rhymes" but rather strength of action and stirring scenes, aided by all available means for producing effect through scenery and the ballet, that he hoped to win success at the Paris grand opera. In the fall of 1838 he began the composition.

The first two acts had scarcely been completed when Paris stood clearly before the poet-composer's eyes. Meanwhile the contract with Holtei drew to a close, but there were difficulties in the way that could not easily be removed. He had contracted many debts and without proof of their liquidation no one could at that time leave Russia. Flight was determined upon. His friend from Koenigsberg, an old and rich lumber merchant, in whose house he had spent many a social evening, took his wife in a carriage over the border, passing her as his own, while Wagner escaped in some other way. At Pillau they went on board a sailing vessel, their first destination being London. Now began the real lifework of Wagner, which was not to cease until he, who had struggled with poverty and sorrow, was to see emperors and kings as guests in his art-temple at Baireuth.

The long sea voyage of twenty-five days, full of mishaps, had a very important bearing upon his art. The stormy sea along the Norwegian coast and the stories of the sailors who never doubled the existence of the "Flying Dutchman," gave life and definite form to the legend. He remained but a short time in London, seeing the city and its two houses of Parliament, and then went to Boulogne-sur-Mer. He remained there four weeks, for Meyerbeer was there taking sea baths, and his Parisian introductions were of the highest importance. The composer of the "Huguenots" immediately recognized the talent of the younger artist, and particularly praised the text to "Rienzi," which Scribe was soon to imitate for him in his weak production of "The Prophet." At the same time he pointed out the obstacles to success in the great city which it would be extremely difficult for one to overcome without means or connections. Wagner however relied on his good star and departed for that city which he conceived to be the only one that could open the way to the stage of the world for a dramatic composer. The result of the visit to Paris was an abundance of disappointments, but it added largely to his experience, increased his strength, nay more, even gave rise to his first great work.

Meyerbeer recommended him to the director of the Renaissance Theatre and besides acquainted him with artists of note. An introduction to the Grand Opera however was out of the question for one who was an utter stranger. Through Heinrich Laube, then in Paris, he made the acquaintance of Heine, who was much surprised that a young musician with his wife and a large Newfoundland dog should come to Paris, where everything, however meritorious, must conquer its position. Wagner himself has described these experiences in Lewald's "Europa," under the title of "Parisian Fatalities of Germans." His first object was to win some immediate success and he accordingly offered to the above named director the "Liebesverbot," which apparently was well suited to French taste. Unfortunately this theatre went into bankruptcy, so all his efforts were fruitless. He now sought to make himself known through lyrics set to music and wrote several, such as Heine's "Grenadiers," but a favorite amateur balladist, Loisa Puget, reigned supreme in the Paris salons, and neither he nor Berlioz could obtain a hearing. His means were constantly diminishing and a terrible bitterness filled his soul against the splendid Paris salons and theatre world, whose interior appeared so hollow.

It happened one day that he heard the Ninth symphony at a performance of the Conservatory, whose concerts were always splendidly and carefully executed, and, as before, it stirred his inmost soul. Once more his genius came to his rescue. He felt intuitively—what we now know with historical certainty—that this work was born of the same spirit which bore Faust, and thus in him also this "ever restless spirit seeking for something new" was called into being and activity. The overture to Faust, in reality the prelude of a Faust symphony, tells us in tones of mighty resolve that his power to do and to will still lived, and would not yield till it had performed its part. This was toward the close of the year 1840.

"The God, who in my breast resides,
Can deeply stir the inner sources;
Though all my energies he guides,
He cannot change external forces.
Thus by the burden of my days oppressed,
Death is desired, and life a thing unblest."

With such a confession he regained strength to battle against Parisian superficiality, which even in the sacred sphere of art seemed to seek only for outward success and to admire whatever fashion dictated. His criticisms on the condition of life and art in Paris are very severe. Even the noble Berlioz does not escape censure from the artist's stand-point, while Liszt, who resided there at the time, he had not yet learned to appreciate. But again the saving genius of his art, German music, rose resplendent, and she it was who recalled him to his own self and to art.

He now entirely gave up the "Liebesverbot," as he felt that he could not respect himself unless he did so. He thought of his native land. A heroic patriotism seized him, although tinged with a political bearing, for he did not forget the Bundestag and its resistance to every movement for liberty, and yet withal he beheld the coming grandeur of his fatherland. Now he himself first fully comprehended Rienzi's words about his noble bride, whom he saw dishonored and defiled, and a deep anger awakened in him those mighty exhorting accents which his enthusiasm had already intoned in Rienzi's first speech to the nobility and the people, and which had not been heard in Germany since Schiller's days. As Rienzi resolved not to rest until his proud Roma was crowned as queen of the world, so now there flashed through him also the conviction, as he has so beautifully said in speaking of Beethoven's music, that the genius of Germany was destined to rescue the mind of man from its deep degradation. In the merely superficial culture, which the Semitic-Gallic spirit had impressed upon the period, and with which it held all Europe as in a net of iron, he saw only utter frivolity. The great revolution had brought about many political and social reforms but the liberation of the soul, like that accomplished by the Reformation, it had not effected. There was a material condition and mental tendency which he afterward, not without reason, compared with the times of the Roman emperors. Heine and his associates formed the literary centre, but even more effective in its influence was Meyerbeer's grand opera. The imperious sway of fashion had usurped the place of real culture and the problem was therefore again to elevate culture with his art to its proper sphere. He became more and more conscious of a mission which went far beyond the realm of mere art-work. Even in this foreign land, which had treated him so coldly and with such hostile egoism, he was to find the ways and means to carry out his mission and to create for us actual human beings instead of phantoms. In his "Parisian Fatalities," Wagner said of the Germans in Paris that they learned anew to appreciate their mother tongue and to strengthen their patriotic feeling. "Rienzi" was an illustration of this patriotic sentiment. He now resolved to produce this composition for Dresden and the thought gave him fresh zeal for work. Elsewhere, he says of the Germans: "As much as they generally dread the return to their native land, they yet pine away from it with homesickness." Longing for home! Had he not once before beheld a being wasting away in the constant longing for the eternal home and yet destined never to find rest? The "Flying Dutchman" recurred to his imagination and to the outward form of the ever-wandering seaman was added the human heart, constantly longing for love and faithfulness. After having come to an understanding with Heine, he rapidly arranged the material of this Wandering Jew of the sea. A fortunate circumstance, the return of Meyerbeer to Paris, even gave promise that the work might secure a hearing at the grand opera.

That he might be at rest while engaged on this work he earned his daily bread by arranging popular operas for cornet-a-piston. He submitted to this deep humiliation for he was conscious of the prize to be obtained by "serving." A partial compensation in thus working for hire he found in the permission given him by the sympathetic music publisher, Schlesinger, to write for his *Gazette Musicale* to which he contributed many brilliant articles. In these he could at least do in words what he was not allowed to do otherwise. He could disclose the splendor of German music, and never before has anyone written of Mozart, Weber, and Beethoven with keener appreciation or profounder thought. Of the last named he proposed to write a comprehensive biography and entered into correspondence with a publisher in Germany.[A] He confronted the formal culture of the Latin races with the character of the German mind, as it were the head of the Medusa, and the consciousness of his mission kept up his spirits under the most trying circumstances. With Paris as an art centre he had done. Like Mozart's "Idomeneo" to the Opera Seria, "Rienzi" was his last tribute to the Grand Opera. They have forever extinguished the genre in style by exhausting its capabilities.

In the meantime "Rienzi" had been accepted at Dresden, and he now hoped through Meyerbeer's influence to see it also accepted by the Grand Opera. The director, however, had been so well pleased with the "Flying Dutchman" that he wished to appropriate the poem for himself, or rather for another composer. In order therefore not to lose everything, Wagner sold the copyright for Paris for 500 francs and it soon after appeared as "Vaisseau Phantome." It naturally followed that for the present his most urgent task was to complete the work for himself and in his own way. The performance of the "Freischuetz" had increased his ambition and his other experiences had completely disgusted him with the modern Babylon. The romance—for such it was—was soon finished. He had allowed a beautiful myth simply to tell its own story and had avoided all the nonsense of the opera with its finales, duets, and ballets, wishing simply to reveal to his countrymen once more the divine attributes of the soul. But now that the romance was to be set to music he feared that his art might have deserted him, so long had it remained unused. However the work progressed rapidly enough. He had in his mind as the main motive of the work, *Senta's* ballad, and around it clustered at once the whole musical arrangement of the material. The Sailor's Chorus and the Spinning Song were popular melodies, for the "Freischuetz" continually kept them humming in his ears. In seven weeks the work was completed, with the exception of the overture, which every day's pressing wants retarded for a few weeks longer.

Leipzig and Munich promptly declined the work with which he had proposed to salute his fatherland once more. The latter city declared that the opera was not adapted to Germany! Through Meyerbeer's influence it was then accepted in Berlin. Thus hated Paris led to the production of two works in which he touched strings that find their fullest response only in a German's heart. The prospect of returning to his fatherland delighted him. What could be more natural than that his mind strove to study more and more closely the spirit and development of his fatherland, in order to raise other and better monuments to it? He renewed his studies in German history, although solely for the purpose of finding suitable material for operas. At first, Manfred and the brilliant era of the Hohenstauffens attracted him. But this historic world at once and utterly disappeared when he beheld that figure in which the spirit of the Ghibellines attained in human form its highest development and greatest beauty—*Tannhaeuser*! His previous readings in German literature had made him familiar with the story, but he now for the first time understood it. The simple popular tale stirred him to such a degree that his whole soul was filled with the image of its hero. It revealed the path to the historic depths of our folk-lore to which Beethoven's and Weber's music had long since given him the clues. The story had some connection with the "Saengerkrieg auf Wartburg," and in this contest, he saw at once the possibility of fully revealing the qualities of his hero, who raises the first German protest against the pretended culture and sham morality of the Latin world. The old poem of this "Saengerkrieg," is further connected with the legend of Lohengrin. Thus it was that in foreign Paris he was destined to gain at once and permanently a realization of the native qualities of our common nature, which, from primeval times, the German spirit has put into these legends.

After a stay of more than three years abroad, he left Paris, April 7, 1842. "For the first time I saw the Rhine; with tears in my eyes, I, a poor artist, swore to be ever loyal to my German fatherland," he says. Have we not seen that this "poor artist" with the might of his magic wand has created a world of new life, and what is far more, has aroused the genius of his people, aye, the very soul of mankind, and has led his epoch and his nation to the achievement of new and permanent intellectual results?

We now come to his first efforts towards the accomplishment of such results. They were to cost hard labor, anxiety, struggles, and pain of every kind indeed, but they were done and they stand to-day.

CHAPTER III.

1842-1849.

REVOLUTION IN LIFE AND ART.

Success and Recognition—Hofkapellmeister to the Saxon Court—New Clouds—"Tannhaeuser" Misunderstood—The Myths of "The Flying Dutchman" and "Tannhaeuser"—Aversion to Meyerbeer—The Religious Element—"Lohengrin"—The Idea of "Lohengrin"—Wagner's Revolutionary Sympathies—The Revolution of 1848—The Poetic Part of "Siegfried's Death"—The Revolt in Dresden—Flight from Dresden— "Siegfried Words."

"Give me a place to stand."—Archimedes.

In an enthusiastic account of the first presentation of the "Flying Dutchman" in Riga, May, 1843, it is said: "The 'Flying Dutchman' is a signal of hope that we shall soon be rescued from this wild wandering in the strange seas of foreign music and shall find once more our blessed home." In a similar strain, the *Illustrierte Zeitung* said: "It is the duty of all who really cherish native art to announce to the fatherland the appearance of a man of such promise as Wagner." Indeed Wagner himself says that the success of the work was an important indication that we need but write "as our native sense suggests." That he himself perceived a new era of the highest and purest outpouring of a new spirit is shown in the composition of this year (1843), the "Liebesmahl der Apostel," wherein he quotes from the Bible: "Be of good cheer for I am near you and My spirit is with you." A chorus of forty male voices exultingly proclaimed this promise from the high church choir loft in Dresden, on the occasion of the Maennergesangvereins-Fest.

"Rienzi" was performed in October 1842, and the "Flying Dutchman" January 2, 1843, both meeting with an enthusiastic reception. Wagner himself had conducted the rehearsals and secured the support of newly won friends and such eminent artists as Schroeder-Devrient and Tichatschek. His success gained for him the distinction of Hofkapellmeister to the Saxon Court. The position once held by Weber was now his. The objects which he had sought to accomplish seemed within reach and he heartily entered into the brilliant art life of the city, the more so as hitherto he had not enjoyed it though possessing the desire and knowledge to do so. Although "Rienzi" retained a certain degree of popularity, the "Flying Dutchman" however had not really been understood, and the more it was heard, the less was it appreciated. How could it be otherwise amid such a public as then existed in Germany? In the upper and middle classes French novels were the favorite literature, while the stage was controlled by French and Italian operas. With all their superficiality they combined perfection in the art of singing, but failed to awaken any sense of the intrinsic worth of our own nature. There were but few of sufficiently delicate feeling to perceive in this composition the continuation of the noble aims of Mozart, Beethoven, and Weber. Wagner himself while in Dresden was destined to continue the struggle against all that was foreign as these three masters had done before him. "Professional musicians admitted my poetic talent, poets conceded that I possessed musical capacity," is the way he characterizes the prevailing misunderstanding of his endeavors and his works, which required a generation to overcome.

He constantly sought to direct public attention to the grander and nobler compositions, such as Gluck's "Armide" and "Iphigenia in Aulis," Weber's "Euryanthe" and "Freischuetz," Marschner's "Hans Heiling," Spohr's "Jessonda," and other grand works for concerts, like Beethoven's "Ninth Symphony" and Bach's "Singet dem Herrn ein neues Lied," all of which were performed in a masterly manner, while such compositions as Spontini's "Vestalin" he at least helped to display in the best light. He was also very active in having Weber's remains brought from London. He not only composed a funeral march, for the obsequies, upon motives from "Euryanthe," which was very powerful in effect, but he also has reminded posterity of what it possesses in this the youngest German master of the musical stage. "No musician, more thoroughly German than thou, has ever lived," he said at the grave. "See, now the Briton does thee justice, the Frenchman admires thee, but the German alone can love thee. Thou art his, a beautiful day in his life, a warm drop of his blood, a part of his heart." Thus at times he succeeded in arousing the public. But on the whole, his ideas were not accepted, and it retained its accustomed views and continued in the old pleasures. Wagner began again to feel more and more his isolated position. The complete misunderstanding of Tannhaeuser, which he began to write when he first arrived in Dresden, and the refusals of the work by other cities, Berlin among them, declaring it "too epic," rendered this sense of isolation complete. The recurrence of such experiences as these showed him how far his art was still removed from its ideal and his contemporaries from the comprehension of their own resources. He realized the fact that his own improved circumstances had deceived him, and that in truth the same superficiality of life and degradation of the stage prevailed everywhere. The course of events during the next generation but proved the truth of this. Whatever of merit was produced met with hostility, as in the case of our artist. The growing perception of these facts led him gradually to revolt against the art-circumstances of his time, and as he became convinced that the condition of art was but the result of the social and political, indeed of the existing mental condition of the people, he at last broke out into open revolution against the entire system. This very agitation of soul, however, became the source of his artistic creations, wherein he attempted to disclose grander ideals and nobler art, and they form therefore, as in the case of every real artist, his own genuine biography. In tracing the origin of his works, we follow the inner current of his life.

Thus far we have availed ourselves of the biographical notes which Wagner, prior to the representation of the "Flying Dutchman," gave to his friend Heinrich Laube for publication in the "Zeitung fuer die elegante Welt." We are now guided further by one of the most stirring spiritual revelations in existence, his "Communication to my Friends," in the year 1851, in that banishment to which his noblest endeavors had brought him, written with his heart's blood, as a preface to the publication of the three opera poems, namely, "Flying Dutchman," "Tannhaeuser" and "Lohengrin." It is the consummation of his artistic as well as human development out of which grew his highest creations.

We must recur to the "Flying Dutchman," whose real name was "Hel Laender," the guide of the deadship, or the fallen sun-bark, which, according to the Teutonic legend, conveyed the heroes to Hel, the region of perpetual night. We shall confine ourselves however to the later version of the middle ages, the only one with which Wagner was familiar. "The form of the 'Flying Dutchman' is the mythic poem of the people; a primeval trait of humanity is expressed in it with heartrending force," Wagner says to those who in spite of Goethe's "Faust" had formed no conception of the vitality, and poetic treasures that lay concealed in the myth. In its general significance the motive is to be considered as the longing for rest from the storms of life. The Greeks symbolized this in Odysseus, who, during his wanderings at sea, longed for his native land, his wife, and home—"On this earth are all my pleasures rooted." Christianity, which recognizes only a spiritual home, reversed this conception in the person of the "Wandering Jew." For this wanderer, condemned eternally to live over again a life, without purpose and without pleasure, and of which he has long since grown weary, there is no deliverance on earth. Nothing remains to him but the longing for death. Toward the close of the middle ages, after the human mind had been satiated with the supernatural, and the revival of vital activity impelled men to new enterprises, this longing disclosed itself most boldly and successfully in the history of the efforts to discover new worlds. An "impetuous desire to perform manly deeds" seized mankind as the earth-encircling, boundless ocean came into view, no longer the closely encircled inland sea of the Greeks. The longing of Odysseus, which in the "Wandering Jew" has grown into longing for death, now aims at a new life, not yet revealed, but distinctly perceived in the prospective. It is the form of the "Flying Dutchman," in which both expressions of the human soul are joined in a new and strange union, such as the spirit of the people alone can produce. He had sworn to sail past a cape in spite of wind and waves, and for that is condemned by a demon, the spirit of these elements, to sail on the ocean through all eternity. He can gratify the longing which he feels, through a woman, who will sacrifice herself for his love, but to the Jew it was denied. He seeks this woman therefore that he may pass away forever. There is this difference however: She is no longer Penelope caring for her home, but woman in general, the loving soul of mankind, which the world has lost in its eager strife to conquer new worlds, and which can only be regained when this strife shall cease and yield to a new activity, truer to human nature.

"From the swamps and floods of my life often emerged the 'Flying Dutchman,' and ever with irresistible attraction. It was the first popular poem which took deep hold of my heart," says Wagner. At this point his career began as a poet, and he ceased to write opera-texts. It is true there was still much that was indecisive and confused in the experiment, but the leading features are pictured verbally with remarkable clearness, and the music invests them with a sense and distinctness of convincing force as an inseparable whole, such as had not been previously known in opera. It may be said that with the "Flying Dutchman" a new operatic era began, or rather the attainment of its dimly conceived destiny as a musical drama. It also expresses the mental activity of the time and the longing for a new world, which was to redeem mankind and secure for us an existence worthy of ourselves. It still appears to us as the native land, encircling us with its intimate associations, and yet there also appears in it the longing for a return to our own individual identity, in which alone we can find the traces of our higher humanity, which a narrowing and degrading foreign influence had banished. Goethe's "Faust," Byron's "Manfred," and Heine's "Ratcliff," all give utterance to the same feeling, with more or less beauty and power; but the blissful repose of deliverance really secured, they could not express with the perfection displayed by Wagner. He was not only secure in this advantage, but he was able to pursue it with increasing energy, so as to push away to a great distance the obstacles which burdened the time.

We perceive the same characteristic in "Tannhaeuser," which, it seems, even at that time had impressed itself upon him with great force. This legend also had its origin in the myths of nature. The Sun-god sinks at eve on Klingsor's mountain castle in the arms of the beautiful Orgeluse, queen of the night, from whose embraces the longing for light drives him again at dawn. We must, however, also here confine ourselves to the particular mediæval form of the legend, as Wagner himself relates it.

The old Teutonic goddess, Holda, whose annual circuit enriched the fields, met the same fate after the introduction of Christianity, as Wotan, that of having her kindly influence suspected and described as malignant. She was relegated to the heart of the mountains, as her appearance was supposed to indicate disaster. At a later period, her name disappeared in that of the heathen Venus, to which all conceptions of a being that entices to evil pleasures could be more easily attached. One such mountain region was the Hoerselberg (Orgelusa Mountain), in Thuringia, where Venus maintained a luxurious, sensual court. Jubilant melodies were heard there, which led him, whose blood ran riot, unwittingly into the mountain. A beautiful old song, however, tells us that the noble knight, Tannhaeuser, mythically the same as Heinrich von Ofterdingen, remained there a whole year, and then was seized with the recollection of the life on earth, and made a pilgrimage to Rome to obtain indulgence for his sins. It reads thus:

"The Pope had a stick white and dry,
Cut from the branches so bare;
Thy sins shall all be forgiven,
When on it green leaves appear."

Tannhaeuser wanders again into the mountain. But the good sense of the people knew what was just:

"To bring consolation to man,
The priest is commissioned of Heaven;
The penitent, sorrowing heart
Hath all its sins forgiven."

The condemnation of the penitent is the curse of the old church, for according to the true doctrine of the Gospels, as accepted and faithfully treasured by the German people after long struggles, it is not deeds but faith that secures salvation. So in the progress of the legend leaves sprout from the dry stick, for "high above the universe is God and his mercy is no mockery."

Wagner gives to the loving Elizabeth the knowledge of this eternal mercy and from a simple child-like being she ascends to the heights of martyrdom. Not until one human soul had gained the strength to die for his redemption is the vehemence of his own nature broken, and he finds relief in death, thus verifying the essence of religion and rejecting forever false church-doctrine.

"A consuming glowing excitement kept my blood and nerves in a state of feverish agitation," Wagner says, speaking of the first presentation of this

"Tannhaeuser." His fortunate change of circumstances, contact with a luxurious court, and the expectation of material success had fostered a desire for pleasure that led him in a direction counter to his real nature. There was no other way to satisfy this craving except by following as an artist the reigning fashion and the general striving after success. "If I were to condense all that is pernicious and wearisome in the making of opera-music, I should call it Meyerbeer," he says, "inasmuch as it ignores the wants of the soul and seeks to gratify the eye and ear alone." After all, was it the mere gratification of the senses that he really longed for? His aspirations grew in the natural soil of those life-feelings which dictate that religion and morality shall not destroy natural impulses, but sanctify them. Before his soul stood a pure, chaste, maidenly image of unapproachable and intangible holiness and loveliness. In his own words, his nature passionately and ardently embraced the outward forms of this conception whose essence was the love of all that is noble and pure. No other artist ever possessed a deeper sense of the need of our time. With this protest against the violence done our purely human nature, he places us again on a solid footing and symbolizes in art the highest accomplishment of religion—regeneration by knowledge. It is to this that we owe the regeneration of our national life. The religious element of our nature has preserved us and made us a great nation.

He confesses he had been so intensely engrossed in composing "Tannhaeuser," that the nearer he approached the end, the more the idea possessed him that sudden death would prevent its completion. As he wrote the last note it seemed to him as though his life had been in danger till then. The "Flying Dutchman" was a protest against the purposeless wanderings of the human mind in every external department of knowledge, while "Tannhaeuser" was a bold historical protest against all that would subject the hidden sense of truth in our nature to violent interpretation and arbitrary dogmas. From this time forth his sphere became the purely human, and in this too he shows us by his powerful art that which is indispensable and eternal in human existence joined with the complete realization of the only natural way to develop all our qualities. We have come to "Lohengrin," conceived in 1847, and completed in its instrumental parts in March, 1848. It was in truth "his child of pain."

After the completion of "Tannhaeuser," his native sense of humor prompted him to design a satirical play on the "Saengerkrieg auf Wartburg," namely the "Meistersinger von Nuernberg," of which, more further on. The painful experience of being misunderstood in all his earnest efforts as a man and as an artist, his failure to make the assistance he longed to give acceptable, drove him back with passionate vehemence into a serious frame of mind, in which condition he could well understand the

Lohengrin material. Hitherto, in the mystic twilight of its mediæval presence, it had inspired him with some degree of suspicion, but he now recognized in it a romance, wherein was embodied the longing desires of pure human nature, and the imperative necessity of love, as well as its artistic meaning.

The fundamental trait of this legend, as in "Tannhaeuser" and in the flight of Odysseus from the embraces of sensualism, had already appeared in the Greek myth of Zeus and Semele. Like the God from the cloudy Olympian realms, so Lohengrin from the boundless ether to which Christian imagination had assigned Olympus, descends to the human female in the natural longing of love. There was an old tradition in the legends of the people who dwelt near the sea, to the effect that on its blue surface an unknown man of indescribable grace and beauty approaches, whose resistless charms win every heart. He disappears again, retreating with the waves, whenever it is sought to discover who he is. So also in the Scheldt region once appeared a handsome hero, drawn by a swan. He rescued a persecuted, innocent maiden, and married her, but when she asked him who he was and whence he came, he was compelled to forsake her. How does our poet interpret the legend?

Lohengrin, the son of Parcival, the royal guardian of the Holy Grail, who represents the ideal in humanity, although he was probably originally identical with the German Sun-god, who longs to rest in the arms of night—this Lohengrin seeks the wife that believes in him, who will not ask who he is and whence he came, but will love him as he is, and simply as he appears to her. He sought the wife, to whom he need not declare himself, need not justify himself, but who will love him without question. Like Zeus, he had to conceal his divine nature, for only in this way could he know that he was really loved, and not simply admired, which was all he longed for when he descended from his ethereal heights to the warm earth below. He longs to be human, to experience the warm feelings of humanity, and gain a loving heart; with these longings he descended from his blissful, lonely heights, when he heard the cry of this heart for help in the midst of mankind. The halo of his higher nature, however, betrays him. He can not but appear as miraculous. The staring of the vulgar and the rancor of the envious cloud the heart of the loving Elsa. Doubts and jealousy show that he has not been understood but simply adored, and this draws from him the confession of his divinity, after which he returns, his purpose unaccomplished, to his solitude.

We must bear in mind how highly our poet even at that time prized this artistic wealth. To Goethe, art was "like good deeds;" Schiller hoped with its aid to unify the nation, and Wagner, especially after the discovery of such grand art-material as those myths contained, regarded it as the real fountain of health for the nation and the time. We shall soon observe that at last his art embraced our highest ideals in religion as well. Such an art, however, exists only in the heart which believes in it, and we have seen how antagonistic was the spirit of the time, particularly to this artist, who had emerged from the blissful solitude of his own creative mind and sought the sympathy of the warm human heart. He justly felt that the theme was a tragic symbol of the time, and he was therefore enabled to present Lohengrin as an entirely new artistic conception, something no poet had previously succeeded in accomplishing.

More than this he discloses to us that which his Elsa imparted to him—the nature of the feminine heart. "I could not help justifying her in the outbreak at last of jealousy and at that moment for the first time I fully comprehended the purely human nature of love," he says. "This woman, who by passion is brought from the heights of rapturous adoration back to her real nature and reveals it in her ruin, this magnificent woman, from whom Lohengrin disappeared because his peculiar nature prevented him from understanding her, I had now discovered." The effect of this was to clarify his vision, as we shall likewise learn. The lost arrow that he sent after this valuable treasure had been his Lohengrin, which he had to sacrifice in order to discover the track of the "true womanly" which Goethe was the first to long for ardently, and which music had revealed as it were the sound of a bell in the dark forest. This alone can explain why the masculine egoism, even in so noble a form as our idealism had hitherto assumed, was forced to yield to its influence. But this Elsa was only the unconscious spirit of the people and the perception of this must of necessity have made him, as he says, "a thorough revolutionist." He felt that this spirit of the people was restrained by wrong conceptions of morality and false ideals. He heard its lamentations, and verily, if ever a genius served his people, then did the genius of Wagner avail him as the worker of "good deeds." He prophetically indicated at that time what subsequently became an exquisite reality. "Only a good deed can help here," he writes after the completion of "Lohengrin." "A gifted and inspired man must with good fortune attain to power and influence who can elevate his inmost convictions to the dignity of law. For it is possible after all, if chance will have it so that a king will permit a competent man to have his way as well as an incompetent one. The public can only be educated through facts. So long as an immense majority is carried away by the mezza-voce of a virtuoso, its needs are readily discerned and satisfied."

It is now our duty to record how he arrived at this remarkably independent action of the artist; we follow his notes, as they furnish the clearest testimony. Their stirring recital is touching enough for any one who can look upon the nation in the light of the history of mankind, to which has been assigned its own peculiar ideal problems.

In the meantime the revolution of 1848 had broken out. Although never really much inclined toward politics, Wagner had foreseen its necessity; but as soon as he came in contact with its various elements, he recognized only too clearly that none of the warring factions had the least conception of his own aims. Notwithstanding this, he perfected a plan for the reorganization of the stage by which alone under the circumstances the nation and the time could be strongly impressed again with the ideal in thought and art. The political rostrum showed soon enough how blunt were its arrows. And what of the Catholic syllabus and Protestant "Culturkampf" as well? Dead children born of dead mothers! Most of all it was important to create anew for that stage the ideals which would serve to elevate the time. Even while at work on "Lohengrin," which always made him feel as if he were on an oasis in a desert waste and for which he gathered strength from the performance of the Ninth symphony in Dresden, Siegfried and Friedrich der Rothbart appeared to him. Each contained the elements which lie nearest the heart. Each was a type and model of our distinct characteristics. He recognized at once however that Friedrich I. (Barbarossa) was only the historical regeneration of Siegfried, and that the latter was in reality the youthful handsome hero to form the object and centre of a work of art and to convey to us in its fullness and beauty the purely human idea as Wagner conceived it. How he found and interpreted this Siegfried, he has told us in the pamphlet, "The Wibelungen, History from Legend" which appeared in 1850.

The delight produced by the discovery of this "actor of reality, this man in the fullness of highest and boundless power and most indisputable loveliness" revealed to him by his Elsa, only intensified for the present at least the feeling that in his best efforts and his knowledge he stood sadly alone. His longing was intense, the more so that in this actual life he could accomplish his purpose as Faust says:

"The God, who in my breast resides,
He can not change external forces."

This longing grew until it seemed as if self-annihilation alone could bring relief, and then appeared to him the image of Him whose death brought salvation to mankind. He conceived the idea of picturing a human "Jesus of Nazareth," to represent the universal rejection, in all its malignity and rancor, to which Jesus fell a victim. The reflection, however, that he certainly could not secure a representation of his work under existing circumstances, and the additional fact that after the Revolution, which seemed bound to destroy every favorable condition, such a declaration of internal struggle would have counted for nothing, induced him to leave the plan unexecuted. Besides, in this year (1848), he had already finished "Siegfried's Death," in its poetic form, and had even sketched some of the musical thoughts connecting with that new world, to which he had looked forward with such buoyant hope. At last came also the complete rupture with the world that surrounded him, even while he was devoting the best endeavors of his life to it. Wagner himself informs us of the clear insight he had gained into the nature of the political movement. Either the old state of things must remain intact or the new must sweep it entirely away. He recognized the approach of the catastrophe which was certain to engulf every one who was in earnest and unselfish enough to desire a change of the deplorable conditions so generally felt. The ancient spirit of a decayed past had outlived itself and openly and insolently offered defiance to the existing and ruling conditions. Knowing well the unavoidable decision which he would have to form, he ceased all productive activity. Every stroke of the pen appeared ridiculous, inasmuch as he could no longer deceive himself in regard to his prospects. He spent these May-days of 1849 in the open air, basking in the sunshine of the awakening spring and casting away all egoistic desires.

At this time the revolt in Dresden occurred, which, as a sort of forlorn hope, he thought might be the beginning of a general uprising in Germany. "After what has been said, who could be so blind as not to see that I had now no choice but to turn my back upon a world, to which no ties of sympathy bound me," he says, thus clearly indicating his active participation in the May-revolt. It was not long before the Prussians appeared, who had only waited the signal from Dresden. With many others Wagner had to take to flight. A long, sad banishment followed, but out of its necessities and privations rose the full man and artist who restored to his nation its ideals, or rather first established the ideal in its perfection. How this conception came to him is disclosed in the last words he uttered about the men and circumstances which combined to wickedly conceal it. It is as bold as it is inspiring, and it is only the deepest solicitude for our most sacred treasures that could give utterance to such words. It reads:

"There is nothing with which to compare the sensation of pleasure I experienced after the first painful impressions had been overcome, when I felt myself free, free from a world of tormenting, ever unsatisfied desires, free from conditions in which my aspirations had been my sole absorbing nourishment. When I, persecuted and proscribed, was no longer bound by any considerations to resort to a deception of any kind; when I had given up every hope and desire, and with unconstrained candor could say openly and plainly that I, the artist, hated from the bottom of my heart this hypocritical world which pretended to be interested in art and culture; when I could say to it that not one drop of artist's blood flowed in all its veins, that it had not one spark of manly culture or manly beauty,—then for the first time in my life I felt myself completely free, happy, and joyous, although I sometimes did not know where to conceal myself the next day that I might still breathe the free air of heaven."

These are words such as a Siegfried might have spoken. From this time on he did not rest until the Siegfried-deed was done and the sword was thrust into the dragon's heart.

The preparations for it were conducted with untiring energy and great wisdom. The works of art which he had already forged were the sword. The true and noble art, which had begun with Goethe, was now introduced in the various European centres of culture "with considerate speed," and finally inspired in Germany, the very centre of this culture and art, an understanding of their real elements. In the modest Zurich where the banishment began, in London—Paris had rejected it—in Petersburg, in Vienna, in Munich, and at last also in Berlin, which at that time did not appear to have "one drop of artist's blood in all its veins" the world's attention was aroused anew by actual representations, though often only in parts, to the fact, that the latter-day art of the last generation had removed us a great distance from our ideals. And finally he succeeded, at first in Munich, subsequently in Baireuth, in securing for the art of the stage a proper representation, and with it an awakening of the age to a correct perception of art as expressive of the ideal which stimulates the whole world. The thrust which pierced the heart of the dragon of the modern theatres was his "Parsifal," and the Siegfried, who dealt the blow, gained with his art the slumbering bride, the re-awakening heart of the nation and mankind.

Who is there to-day who will doubt that Faust denial of the curse and the prophetic presentment of a new world? Is it not true that the governing powers of the present time have seized upon the ideas in politics and society, which were the kernel of the movement of 1848 and 1849? Whenever they shall understand the mental strivings of the nation, as well as the political and military, then art and religion will gain the dignity and the right to which they are entitled. The revolt of Wagner was the revolt of the better soul of the nation which had been estranged from itself. Thirty years of deeds have shown that his word was the truth. We now come to their recital.

CHAPTER IV.

1850-1861.

EXILE.

Visit to Liszt—Flight to Foreign Lands—Three Pamphlets—"Lohengrin" Performed—Wagner's Musical Ideas Expressed in Words—Resumption of the Nibelungen Poem—The Idea of the Poem—Its Religious Element— The First Music-Drama—In Zurich—New Art Ideas—Increasing Fame— "Tristan and Isolde"—Analysis of this Work—In Paris Again—The Amnesty—Tannhaeuser at the "Grand Opera"—"Lohengrin" in Vienna— Resurrection of the "Mastersingers of Nuremberg"—Final Return to Germany.

Seeking with all the soul the Grecian land.—Goethe.

The first impression following his sudden change of fate appeared in Wagner's own world as a good omen. "What I felt as I conceived this music, he felt when he conducted it; what I intended to say as I wrote it, he said as he interpreted it," he says of the Tannhaeuser rehearsal under Liszt's direction in Weimar, where he had gone for a few days for the sake of this "rarest of friends," who had already of his own accord given "Rienzi" and "Tannhaeuser" in the small Thuringian court-residence to which the Wartburg belongs.

His stay was cut short however, and disguised as a waggoner he left the city. Unfortunately the only place which he could reach in safety was Paris, and from this city he also speedily fled as from a dismal spectre whose disgusting features were again recognized. And yet he was destined to return to it, to retrieve his fortunes, with a possible success as an opera-composer, but also to be permanently convinced that this "modern Babylon," where others had conquered the world with their art-substitutes, was in absolute contrast with that which he sought and needed for his labors. But of Weimar he exclaimed:

"How wonderful! By the love of this rarest of friends, in the time when I was homeless, I secured the long desired and true home for my art, which I had hitherto sought in vain elsewhere. When I was doomed to wander in foreign lands, he who had wandered so much, retired permanently to a small town and there provided me a home."

Liszt had given up entirely his career as a performer, and acted mainly as Hofkapellmeister at the grand-ducal court in Weimar. Wagner made his acquaintance "in the terrible Parisian past," but did not then understand him. Liszt, however, lovingly watched his progress like an elder brother, and drew the misunderstood genius to his great heart. "Everywhere and always he cared for me. Ever prompt and decisive where aid was required, with a cordial response to all my wishes, and devoted love for me, he was to me what I had never found before, and with that intensity whose fullness we only comprehend when it actually embraces us in all its vastness."

Among the inspiring mountains of Switzerland he wrote a protest against the pretense of the momentary victors of the revolution, that they were the protectors of art. His pamphlet, "Art and the Revolution," disclosed the real nature of this so called art in the unsettled political and social condition of the time, and energetically rejected as art anything which under any guise sought to speculate upon the public. The "Art-Work of the Future" was a more extended paper which described the deadly influence of modern fashion upon art itself and the egoistic dismemberment of it into distinct branches, and revealed the art of the future as embracing all human art-capacities.

This misunderstood assertion gave rise to the term, "music of the future," first used by a would-be professor, L. Bischoff in Cologne, and immediately repeated everywhere by the thoughtless multitude. In the first pamphlet he assailed the governments which only sought their own particular advantage. In the second, likewise misunderstood, he irritated all the artists. His fiercest indignation was expended upon the born arch-enemies of our art and culture in the same year, 1850, when he published "Judaism in Music," under the name of "Freigedank." "What the heroes of the fine arts have wrested in the course of two thousand unhappy years of strenuous and persistent efforts, from the demon hostile to art, the Jew to-day converts into drafts on art-merchandise. Who would imagine that this great work has been cemented with the sweat and toil of genius for two thousand years," he exclaims in the exasperation of his soul at these flippant time-servers who dominated in the concert-hall and on the stage. Naturally the legion of their followers did not become his friends. They controlled the press, and it is due to this, that his most important writings are known even to-day only by his friends.

About this time he wrote the poetry to "Wiland der Schmied." It was in Paris he showed the Germans how dire necessity contrives the wings with which to escape from bondage and regain sweet liberty. Under the peculiar constraint which work, foreign to his nature, imposed upon him and which made him sick in body and soul, his eyes one day fell upon the score of "Lohengrin." Two words to Liszt and the reply determined him upon its performance. It occurred, August 28, 1850. It was in fact a fresh protest against a false art-world and in 1870, when the German people stood arrayed in arms against our foreign enemy everyone exclaimed in astonishment, "Lohengrin!" This selection for the celebration of Goethe's birthday was worthy of his memory, for Wagner, as great a poet as he was musician, had invested the work with every charm of tragic beauty, both in the text and poetical construction as well as in the ingenious design of its dramatic situations. The work marks a notable era in the history of German music.

Wagner now fully explained in his book, "Opera and Drama," published in 1861, the object of his art-revolution. The opera hitherto, as he said, was not even the germ, how much less the fruit of the art-work he purposed. On the contrary, the methods hitherto applied must be completely changed. Music must be made the essential and highest method of expression of poetry and the drama; but not the principal theme to which words and situations are subordinated. In this he unfolded all his artistic experience and claimed that whoever failed to understand him now, did so because he was determined not to understand. This can be found more fully treated in the "Allgemeine Musikgeschichte." To his real friends he presented in the autumn of the same year that "Communication" which reveals to us his manhood and is a biography of the soul without parallel.

The high purpose, perceivable from afar, whither his endeavors tended, appears in the real work of our artist taken up again at last. The noble and affectionate regard of the family of the rich merchant Wesendonck, in Zurich, provided him with a pleasant place of rest and needed support. The performance of "Lohengrin" was a summons to new deeds. He resumed the Nibelungen poem, and we shall see its powerful influence upon the national spirit and national art.

"Man receives his first impressions from surrounding nature, and in it no effect is so strong as that of light." Thus he begins in the "Wibelungen" of 1850. The day, the sun, appears as the very condition of life. Praise and adoration are bestowed upon it in contrast with the dark night which breeds terror. Thus light becomes the cause of all existence, Father, God. The day-break appears as the victory of light, and naturally there grow out of it at last moral impressions. This influence of nature is the foundation of all conceptions of divinity, the division into distinct religions depending upon the character of different tribes. The tribal tradition of the Franks, as the noblest type of the Germans, has the advantage of a steady development from its ancient origin into historic life. It likewise shows us in the far distant past the individual God of light as he slays the monster of the chaotic night—Siegfried's struggle with the dragon.

But as the day surrenders to the night and summer is followed by winter, so Siegfried finally is conquered and the god is changed into mortal man. Now that he has fallen, he kindles in the human heart a deeper sympathy. As the victim of a struggle that enriches us, he arouses the moral sense of vengeance against the murderer. The primeval struggle in nature is therefore continued by ourselves and its success is seen in the vicissitudes of human life through the ages, moving on from life to death, from joy to grief, and thus in perpetual rejuvenescence clearly discloses the character of man as well as of nature. The embodiment of this constant motion, the active life itself, however, ultimately finds in Wotan (Zeus) as the father of light, its distinct form. Although Zeus reigned supreme as the father of all the gods, yet his origin is due to the advanced knowledge of man while the God of light, Siegfried, is natural and so to speak born with him.

"The most important part of this tribal legend of the Franks is the treasure which Siegfried obtains and which henceforth bears his attributes as opposed to those of the primeval myth. The Scandinavians, for instance, have preserved a Nifelheim as the abode of the black demigods in contrast to the demigods of light. These Niflungars, children of night and of death, search the interior of the earth, discover its hidden treasures and invest them with new life by forging them into weapons and ornaments. The Nibelungs, whom we also find as the Myrmidons accompanying Achilles, the Siegfried of the Greeks—are now with their treasure elevated by the Franks to a moral importance. When Siegfried slew the Nibelungen dragon he gained its treasure. The possession of it increases his power immeasurably inasmuch as he now commands the Nibelungs, but it is at the same time the cause of his death, for the heir of the dragon seeks to regain the treasure and treacherously slays him as night does the day and draws him into the dark realm of death. Siegfried is transformed into a Nibelung! Although the acquisition of the treasure dooms it to death, still each new generation inevitably strives to obtain it. The treasure represents the embodiment of worldly power. It is the earth with all its glory as we see it at dawn, our own sunny property after the night has been driven away which had spread its dragon wings like a horrid spectre over the rich treasures of the world.

"The treasure itself, which the Nibelungs have gathered, is the metal found in the bowels of the earth which enables us to improve the earth, and to fashion weapons and golden crowns, the means of power and its symbols. The divine hero Siegfried, who first obtained it and thus became a Nibelung, left to his race the claim to the treasure. To revenge the slain hero and regain the treasure is the aim of the whole race of the Nibelung-Franks, and by it they are recognized in history as well as in legend."

Accordingly we find the noblest hero of the "Wibelungen," Friedrich Barbarossa, of the Hohenstauffen race ruling in the mountain, surrounded by Wotan's ravens. It is possible that the Franks were the ruling tribe even in the Indo-germanic home; at all events they laid claim to the mastery of the world as soon as they appear in history. Of this impulse or desire Charlemagne must have been conscious when he gathered the old tribal songs which contained the religious ideas of the race. Upon it Napoleon based his claim to the realm of Charlemagne. Is it not even possible that the Hohenzollerns were influenced by the recollection of this Germanic past when they endeavored to regain their old tribal seat in the Hohenstauffen land?

Here we close the intimate connection of the Nibelungen legend with our history. Temporal power, however, is not the highest destiny of a civilizing people. That our ancestors were conscious of this is shown in the fact that the treasure, or gold, and its power, was transformed into the Holy Grail. Worldly aims gave place to spiritual desires. With this interpretation of the Nibelungen myth, Wagner acknowledged the grand and eternal truth that this life is tragic throughout, and that the will which would mould a world to accord with one's desires can finally lead to no greater satisfaction than to break itself in a noble death. This latter truth, which even the ancient Orient saw clearly when in its history the Lord himself breaks the self-will of Jacob in a dream, moves as a deep consciousness through the Germanic myths, and induced the Germans to accept not only the higher faith developed from such a basis to which alone they owe the preservation of their impetuous activity, but also tended to give this Christian truth itself a wider and deeper significance. In their myths they had already indicated that the possession of this world is not the only thing to be desired. They have the world-devastation, Muspilli, the "Twilight of the Gods." It is this conquering of the world through the victory of self which Wagner conveys as the highest interpretation of our national myths. As Brunhilde approaches the funeral pyre to sacrifice to the beloved dead, Siegfried, the life—the only tie which still binds her to this earth—she says:

"If, like a breath, the gods disappear,
Without a pilot the world I leave.
To the world I will give now my holiest wisdom:
Not goods, nor gold, nor god-like pomp,
Not house, nor lands, nor lordly state,
Not wicked plottings of crafty men,
Not base deceits of cunning law,—
But, blest in joy and sorrow let only love exist."

Such was the "Ring of the Nibelungen" which Wagner created out of the vast collection of German legends and not merely out of the distinctively national Nibelungen epic. The completion of "Siegfried's death," now the "Goetterdaemmerung," led to Siegfried's "Schwertschmiedung," (Sword-wielding); "Drachenkampf," (Dragon-struggle) and "Brautgewinnung," (Bride-winning) and further investigation of the subject led him in the

"Walkuere" to picture Brunhilde's guilt and punishment, and finally in the "Rheingold" a psychological foundation for the whole. The work took this mental shape as early as 1851. Two years later, the poem, for which he had chosen the alliterative style of the Edda as the only suitable form, was given to his friends, and in 1863 to the world. From that time his sole ambition was to bring this first all-comprehensive German national drama into life by having it performed as a distinct festival-play far from the everyday theatre. Nearly twenty years elapsed between this and the realization of the idea. But why take note of time when great and grand things are to be accomplished?

The following decade brought with it many changes to Wagner, without however at any time diverting his mind from the purpose of his life, which constantly became clearer. Every opportunity was improved to direct attention and approach nearer to it. The death of Spontini gave occasion to a memorial tribute, closing with the words: "Let us bow reverently before the grave of the creator of the 'Vestalin,' 'Cortez,' and 'Olympia.'" He sought with operas and concerts to develop the limited musical resources of Zurich, where he had taken up his permanent residence, because he had always met with a most cordial personal reception there. In this he was aided by scholars who came to him from Germany, most prominent among whom was Hans von Buelow, who had been in Weimar with Liszt, and had become enthusiastic over "Lohengrin." Wagner overcame his own repugnance to the operas of Meyerbeer and his associates, which he hoped his "Lohengrin" was destined to obliterate, and directed their performance. To do the same for his own works, the requisite strength was lacking. "Some of us are old, others are young. Let the older one think not of himself, but let him love the younger for the sake of the inheritance which he places in his heart to cherish anew, for the day will come when the same shall be proclaimed for the welfare of humanity the world over," are the closing words of his "Opera and Drama." He found consolation and compensation in performing the symphonies of Beethoven, for two of which he prepared a special program; but as he desired to have the real motives of his work understood by the hospitable little city, he wrote a pamphlet, "A Theatre in Zurich," wherein he advocated the establishment and maintenance of a theatre by the citizens themselves, as the Greeks had done. It was another evidence of his firm conviction that the stage had a high mission in the culture of our time. He even lectured on the subject of dramatic music, and recited the poem of "Siegfried's Death," which made a profound impression.

Very soon thereafter appeared the remarkable "Letter to Liszt in Regard to the Goethe Memorial," wherein he confidently asserted that painter as well as sculptor would decline to compete with the poet acting in harmony with the musician, and that they would with reverential awe bow before an art-work in comparison with which their own productions would seem but lifeless fragments. For such an art-work there should therefore be prepared a suitable place rather than continue contributions to the support of the individual arts, which the former would invigorate and elevate anew. We see to-day that the plastic arts also strike out in new paths. Liszt and Wagner have inspired their epoch and the sculptor Zumbusch in Vienna has given us their busts. In a similar strain he challenged musical criticism and thereupon began with the gradual spread of "Tannhaeuser," and soon also of "Lohengrin," those seemingly endless disputes which, however, at the same time increased the strength of some younger men, among whom were Uhlig, Pohl, Cornelius, Raff and Ambros. These practical performances, as little as they presented an artistic ensemble, yet tended to arouse and shape talents that Wagner could avail himself of later for his own higher purposes. Among them were Milde and his wife, Ander, Schnorr, Formes, Niemann and Beck. Wagner's niece Johanna, was already familiar with his method from her Dresden experience. He endeavored in a pamphlet discussing the way to perform "Tannhaeuser" to rescue it from banishment and familiarize the artists with its merits but they remained deaf or hostile. He became absorbed the more in his Nibelungen-poem, leaving to his good genius his deliverance from external isolation. And yet the latter became a source of pleasure when, in the manner of von Eschenbach's Parcival, who also presented the sorrows and deeds of the mythical sun-hero, familiar to him since 1845, he undertook to portray the forest-solitude in which his young Siegfried grew up and gained all the miraculous power of nature, above all, that inner confidence which banishes fear from the human breast.

A brighter future seemed to open when, notwithstanding the doubts of his friends of the ultimate success of his "monstrous undertaking," the knowledge of which began to spread, the German artists generally accepted his invitation to spend a Wagner week in Zurich, and parts of his masterly works were performed with such effect that "the amiable maestro stood buried in flowers." For the overture to the "Flying Dutchman," as well as for the prelude to "Lohengrin," he composed an explanatory introduction.

In the autumn of the same year he was in Italy, and, lying sleepless in a hotel at La Speccia, he found for the first time those plastic "nature-motives" which in the Nibelungen-trilogy with constantly increasing individuality are made the exponents of the passions and the characters which give expression to them. He immediately returned to his dreary, involuntary home to proceed with the completion of his colossal work, which was to engage his attention for many years. A visit from Liszt, in October, led to a profounder understanding of Beethoven's last sonatas, so that their language was fully identified with his own. "Rheingold" and the "Walkuere" were soon finished.

His fame meanwhile grew steadily. He received an invitation for the concerts of the Philharmonic society in London, for which Beethoven had written the Ninth Symphony and designed the Tenth, which, according to his Sketches, was to show what all great poetic minds longed for—the union of the tragic spirit of the Greeks with the religious of the modern world. It was the same high goal that Wagner touched in the "Nibelungenring" and attained in "Parcival." The English at that time were even less disposed to appreciate his efforts than the Germans, and the Jewish spirit of their church inclined them to look with suspicion upon the "Jew Persecutor." He also found at first some difficulties in the rushing style of execution, which was a tradition from Mendelssohn, who was idolized in England. His untiring energy, however, prevailed everywhere where art was at stake, and the last of the eight concerts, in which Mozart's C Major Symphony and Beethoven's Eighth were given, and the "Tannhaeuser Overture," was encored, brought him, in a storm of applause, compensation for the unworthy calumniations of the press, notably, of the *Times*. Notwithstanding all this, he could not be induced to re-visit London till twenty years later. The invitations from America he declined at once.

His art-susceptibility at that time was very keen and active. He remarked to a German admirer, in the autumn of 1856, that two new subjects occupied his mind during the Nibelungen-work, which he could with difficulty repress. The one was "Tristan," with which Gottfried's brilliant epic had already made him familiar in composing the "Walkuere," and the other, probably, was "Parcival," whose Good Friday enchantment had impressed him many years before. In October Liszt visited him again, and heard the "Walkuere" on the piano. A musical journal in Leipzig was emboldened to speak of a forthcoming event that would agitate the whole musical world. With what joyous cheerfulness he composed "Siegfried," and his Anvil-song is shown in a letter about Liszt's symphonic poems, which appeared in the following spring. Accident and irresistible impulse, however, led immediately to the completion of "Tristan and Isolde."

The seeming hopelessness of success in his endeavors at times discouraged him. "When I thus laid down one score after the other, never again to take them up, I seemed to myself like a sleep-walker who is unconscious of his actions," he states. And yet he had to seek the "daylight" of the German opera, from which he had fled with his Nibelungen, if he would remain familiar with the active life of his art. He proposed therefore to arrange the much simpler Tristan material within the compass of ordinary stage representation. Curiously enough he received just then an offer to compose an opera for the excellent Italian troupe in Rio Janeiro. He thought, however, of Strasbourg, and it was only through Edward Devrient, who visited him in the summer of 1857, that he destined the work for Carlsruhe where Grand Duke Frederick and his wife, Princess Louisa of Prussia, displayed a growing interest in art. It was also the home of an excellent singer, Ludwig Schnorr from Carolsfeld, of whom Tichatschek had already informed him and who was to be the first to assume the role of Tristan.

"Tristan" belongs, like "Siegfried" and "Parcival," to the circle of the sun-heroes of the primeval myth. He also is forced to use deception and is compelled to deliver his own bride to his friend, then to discern his danger and voluntarily disappear. Thus Wagner remained within his poetic sphere. But while in "Siegfried" the Nibelungen-myth in its historic relations had to be maintained and only the sudden destruction of the hero through the vengeance of the woman who sacrifices herself with him, could be used in "Tristan," on the other hand the main subject lies in the torture of love. The two lovers become conscious of their mutual love through the drinking of the love-potion that dooms them to death. It is a death preferred to life without each other. What in "Siegfried" is but a moment of decisive vehemence appears here in psychological action of endless variety, wherein Wagner has woven the whole tragic nature of our existence, which he had learned from the great philosopher Schopenhauer, to esteem as a "blessing." There was however in this similarity, and at the same time difference, a peculiar charm which invested the work. It is supplementary to the Nibelungen-material which in reality embraces human life in all its relations.

It is wonderful how readily he found the means to unfold before our eyes the revelation which involved the death of the two lovers. Commissioned by his uncle, King Marke, Tristan has conquered the tributary Celts and slain their leader, Morold, in battle. Isolde, the betrothed of the latter, to whose care the wounded Tristan is consigned, is completely captivated when at last her eyes meet his, but unconscious of this he wooes the beautiful woman for the "wearied King" and conducts her to him. Inwardly aroused by this and the death of her former lover, she plans to kill him and while yet on the vessel offers him the cup of poison in retaliation for the slain Morold. Here Brangaene appears and secretly changes the draught so that these two who imagine they had drunk a coming death in which all love should pass away, in this fancied final moment became conscious of life, and confess to each other that love with which they cannot part. It is therefore not the drink in itself but the certainty that death will ensue, which relieves them from constraint. The act of drinking betokens only the moment of consciousness and confession. Nevertheless they cannot live, now that King Marke has discovered their love. Tristan raises himself from the couch where he lies suffering from the wound inflicted by the King's "friend" and tearing open the wound with his own hand, embraces the approaching Isolde, who is now in death united with him forever.

While composing the work, which the prospect of speedy representation hastened forward rapidly, and which he hoped would secure for him a temporary return to his fatherland, an agreeable sensation of complete unrestraint seized him. With utter abandon he could reach the very depths of those soul-emotions which are the very essence of music, and fearlessly shape from them the external form as well. Now he could apply the strictest rules. He even felt, in the midst of his work, that he surpassed his own system. The impressive second act was projected in Venice, where he spent the winter of 1858-59, owing to ill-health. Thence he removed to Lucerne.

From his native land new rays of hope meanwhile penetrated his retirement. Not only Carlsruhe but Vienna and Weimar now grew interested. He ardently longed to strengthen himself, by hearing his own music. "I dread to remain much longer, perhaps, the only German who has not heard my 'Lohengrin,'" he writes to Berlioz, in 1859. He begged permission to return, and sought the intervention of the grand-duke of Baden, as otherwise he would have to go to Paris. The grand-duke took all possible steps to help him, but it was of no avail. His efforts failed, he says, because of the obstinate opposition of the King of Saxony, but it was probably due more to the dislike the unhappy minister, von Beust, himself an amateur composer, entertained for the author-composer. Wagner, therefore, in the autumn of 1859, again went to hated Paris, where he could, at least occasionally, hear good music.

He found in Paris a few really devoted friends of his art as well as of himself, who promised to make his stay home-like in this respect at least. They were Villot, Champfleury, Baudelaire, the young physician Gasperini, and Ollivier, Liszt's son-in-law. The press, however, commenced at once its vicious and corrupt practices against the "musical Marat." Wagner replied with actions. He invited German singers and in three concerts performed selections from his compositions. The beau monde of Paris attended, and the applause was universal, especially after the Lohengrin Bridal-Chorus. The critics however remained indifferent and even malicious. At this juncture, at the solicitation of some members of the German legation, particularly the young princess Metternich, Napoleon gave the order for the performance of "Tannhaeuser," in the Grand Opera-house, much to Wagner's surprise. It must have caused a curious mixture of joy and anxiety in the artist's breast. Standing on the soil of France, he, for the first time, was destined to conquer his fatherland, but on a spot which belonged to the "Grand Opera," and where all the inartistic qualities were fostered that he endeavored to supplant. As his native land was closed to him, he went to work with his usual earnestness, and, as though it were a reward for his faithfulness, there came during the preparations the long-desired amnesty, with the exclusion, however, of Saxony.

In the summer of 1860 he availed himself of his regained liberty to make an excursion to the Rhine and then returned to the rehearsals. Niemann, cast in an heroic mould, had been secured for the title-role. For the instruction of the public he wrote the letter about the "Music of the Future" adopting the current witty expression, which appeared as preface to a translation of his four completed lyric works, exclusive of the Nibelungen-Ring. With admirable clearness he disclosed the purpose of his work. The press on the other hand made use of every agency at its disposal to prejudice Paris from the start against the work. To aggravate matters, Wagner would not consent to introduce in the second act the customary ballet which always formed the chief attraction for the Jockey-club, whose members belonged to the highest society. He simply gave to the scene in the Venusberg greater animation and color. It was for this reason that the press and this club, the malicious Semitic and unintelligent Gallic elements, the former unfortunately of German origin, united in the effort to make the work a failure when presented in the spring of 1861. The history of art discloses nothing more discreditable. The gentlemen of the Jockey-club with their dog-whistles in spite of the protests of the audience succeeded in making the performances impossible and the press declared the work merited such a fate! Wagner withdrew it after the third performance and thereby incurred a heavy debt which it required years of privation to liquidate. At the same time as far as he personally was concerned the occurrence gave rise to a feeling of joyous exaltation. The affair caused considerable excitement and brought him, as he says, "into very important relations with the most estimable and amiable elements of the French mind," and he discovered that his ideal, being purely human, found followers everywhere. The performances themselves could not have pleased him. "May all their insufficiencies remain covered with the dust of those three battle-evenings," he wrote shortly after to Germany.

He realized afresh that for the present his native land alone was the place for a worthy presentation of his music and the enthusiasm which he witnessed at a performance of "Lohengrin" in Vienna, then the German imperial city, convinced him that the insult which had just been offered to the German spirit was keenly felt. Vienna as well as Carlsruhe now requested "Tristan," but the request was not conceded. At a musicians' union which met in Weimar in August, 1861, under Liszt's leadership, Wagner found that the better part of the German artists had also measurably been converted to his views. These experiences and the hope that with a humorous theme selected from German life he might finally obtain possession of the domestic stage and speak heart to heart to his dearly loved people and remind them that even their every day life ought to be transfused with the spirit of the ideal, prompted him to resurrect his "Mastersingers of Nuremberg." It was in foreign Paris that he wrote, in the winter of 1862, the prize song of German life and art which enchants every true German heart. This was the last work he created in a foreign land and in a certain sense he freed himself with it from the sad recollections of a banishment endured for more than ten years to reappear now "sound and serene" before his nation. That this would finally come to pass had always been his last star of hope. "To the Pleiades and to Bootes" Beethoven had likewise marked in his copy of the Odyssey.

We close therefore this chapter of banishment and dire misfortunes with the prospect of a brighter future by communicating the plan of the text of that work as he had already framed it in 1845.

"I conceived Hans Sachs to be the last appearance of the artistic spirit of the people" he says, "and placed him in opposition to the narrow-minded citizens from whom the Mastersingers were chosen. To their ridiculous pedantry, I gave personal expression in the Marker whose duty it was to pay attention to the mistakes of the singers, especially of those who were candidates for admission to the guild." Whenever a certain number of errors had been committed the singer had to step down and was declared unworthy of the distinction he sought. The eldest member of the guild now offered the hand of his young daughter to that master who should win the prize at the public song-festival.

The Marker, who already is a suitor, finds a rival in the person of a young nobleman who, inspired by heroic tales and the minnesingers' deeds, leaves his ruined ancestral castle to learn the art of the mastersingers in Nuremberg. He announces himself for admission prompted mainly by his sudden and growing love for the prize-maiden who can only be gained by a "master." At the examination he sings an inspired song which however gives constant offense to the Marker, so much so, that before he is half through he has exhausted the limit of errors. Sachs, who is pleased with the young nobleman, for his own welfare frustrates the desperate attempt to elope with the maiden. In doing this he finds at the same time an opportunity to greatly vex the Marker. The latter, who to humiliate Sachs had upbraided him because of a pair of shoes which were not yet ready, posts himself at night before the window of the maiden and sings his song as a test, for it is important to gain her vote upon which rests the final decision when the prize is bestowed. Sachs, whose workshop lies opposite the house for which the serenade is intended, when the Marker opens, begins to sing loudly also because as he declares to the irate serenader, this is necessary for him, if he would remain awake while at work so late, and that the work is urgent none knows better than he who had so harshly rebuked him for tardiness. At last he promises to desist, on condition however that he be permitted to indicate the errors which, after his own feeling, he may find in the song, by striking with the hammer upon the last. The Marker sings, Sachs repeatedly and vigorously strikes the last, and the Marker jumps up angrily but is met with the question whether he is through with the song. "Far from it," he cries. Sachs now laughingly hands him his shoes and declares that the strokes of disapproval sufficed to complete them. With the rest of the song, which in desperation he sings without stopping, he lamentably fails before the female form at the window who shakes her head violently in disapproval, and, to add to his own misfortune, he receives a thrashing at the hands of the apprentices and journeymen whom the noise has roused from slumber. The following day, deeply dejected, he asks Sachs for one of his own songs. Sachs gives him one of the young nobleman's poems, pretending not to know whence it came. He cautions him to observe the melody to which it must be sung. The vain Marker, however, believes himself perfectly secure in this, and now sings the poem before the public master and peoples-court to a melody which completely disfigures it, so that he fails again, and this time decisively. Rendered furious, he accuses Sachs of deceit in that he gave him an abominable poem. Sachs declares the poem to be quite good, but that it must be sung according to the proper melody. It is now determined that whoever knows this melody shall be the victor. The young nobleman sings it and secures the bride. The admission into the guild however he declines. Thereupon Hans Sachs humorously defends the mastersingers and closes with the rhyme:

"The Holy Roman Empire may depart,
Yet will remain our Holy German art."

A few years later the German empire arose to new glory and blessing, and yet a lustrum, and with the rise of Baireuth, came the German art.

CHAPTER V.

1862-1868.

MUNICH.

Successful Concerts—Plans for a New Theatre—Offenbach's Music Preferred—Concerts Again—New Hindrances and Disappointments— King Louis of Bavaria—Rescue and Hope—New Life—Schnorr— "Tannhaeuser" Reproduced—Great Performance of "Tristan"— Enthusiastic Applause—Death of Schnorr—Opposition of the Munich Public—Unfair Attacks Upon Wagner—He Goes to Switzerland—The "Meistersinger"—The Rehearsals—The Successful Performance— Criticisms.

O, thus descendest thou at last to me,
Fulfilment, fairest daughter of the Gods.—Goethe.

The pressure of circumstances, as well as the natural desire, to break ground for himself and his new creations, induced him for a time to give concerts with selections from them. He met with marked success before the unprejudiced hearers of Vienna, Prague, St. Petersburg, and Moscow. His visit to Russia especially yielded him a handsome sum, with which he returned to Vienna to await the representation of "Tristan," but owing to the physical inability of Ander, the work finally had to be laid aside. Wagner felt also that intelligence as well as good-will for the cause were lacking; even the Isolde-Dustman did not at heart believe in it. "To speak frankly, I had enough of it and thought no more about it," he tells us.

During this time he published the Nibelungen-poem, and in April, 1863, wrote the celebrated preface which eventually led to the consummation of his desires. He had with Semper conceived the design of a theatre which after the Grecian style should confine the attention of the entire audience to the stage, by its amphitheatric form, thus rendering impossible the mutual staring of the public or at least making it less likely to occur. Because of the oft repeated experience of the deeper effect of music when heard unseen, the orchestra was to be placed so low that no spectator could see the movements of the performers, while at the same time it would result in the more complete harmony of sound from the many and various instruments. In such a place, consecrated to art alone and not to pleasure of the eye, the "stage-festival-play" was to be produced. But would it be possible for lovers of art to provide the means, or was there perhaps a prince willing to spend for this purpose only as much as the maintenance for a short period of his imperfect Opera-house cost him? "In the beginning was the deed," he says with *Faust*, and adds sadly enough in a postscript: "I no longer expect to live to see the representation of my stage-festival-play, and can barely hope to find sufficient leisure and desire to complete the musical composition."

He next thought that the court Opera-house in process of erection in Vienna might be utilized by limiting the number of performances and securing a careful representation of the style of the works produced. Had not Joseph II. recognized the theatre as "contributing to the refinement of manners and of taste"? He even offered to prepare specially for Vienna a more condensed work, the "Meistersingers." The reply was, however, that the name of Wagner had for the present received sufficient consideration, and that it was time to give a hearing to some other composer. "This other name was Jacques Offenbach," adds Wagner. It needs no comment.

Again followed concerts, first in Prague, where "Tristan" was requested, then in Carlsruhe, where he had long been forgotten, although the prince's own love for art had not been extinguished. The Carlsruhe and Mannheim orchestras acknowledged that they now first fully realized that they were artists. A negotiation for permanent settlement at the grand-ducal court failed, owing to the opposition of the courtiers. Wagner had demanded a court-carriage! Frederick the Great has said, it is true, that geniuses rank with sovereigns; but then this was too much, too much! Then too, he had, O horror! spent the beautiful ducats which the grand-duke had presented him, in entertaining of an evening the musicians who had executed the work. Where would such pretensions, such extravagance lead? The same courtiers, however, did not consider it robbery for many years shamefully to abridge the income of their noble prince until they finally stood disgraced themselves and escaped punishment only through the inexhaustible kindness of their monarch.

In Loewenberg, in Breslau, and again in Vienna, everywhere Wagner met with abundant success. But what of the real goal? "The public met him with enthusiasm wherever he showed himself, but on the other hand the leading critics remained cold or hostile and the directors of the theatres closed their doors to him," his biographer, Glasenapp, says truthfully enough. Of the Nibelungen-poem also no notice had been taken except in a very narrow circle. Here and there a copy of the little volume, bound in red and gold, could be found, but the owner was sure to belong to the school of Liszt or Wagner. "How could the poetic work of an opera-composer bear serious consideration in contrast with the elaborate literary productions of professional poets?" Wagner says with justice. He felt himself rejected everywhere, and just where alone he desired admission.

"For me there shone no star that did not pale,
No cheering hope of which I was not reft;
To the world's whim, changing with every gale,
And all its vain caprices, I was left;
To nobler art my aspirations soared,
Yet I must sink them to the common horde.

"He that our heads had crowned with laurels green,
By priestly staff whose verdure had decayed,
Robbed me of Hope's sweet solaces, and e'en
The last delusive comfort caused to fade;
Yet thus was nourished in my soul serene
An inward trust, by which my faith was stayed;
And if to this trust I prove ever true
The withered staff shall blossom forth anew.

"What deep in my own heart I did discern,
Dwelt also, silent, in another's breast;
And that which in his eager soul did burn,
Within my youthful heart peaceful did rest;
And as he half unconsciously did yearn
For all the Spring-time joys that were in quest,
The Spring's delightsomeness our souls shall nourish,
And newer verdure round our faiths shall flourish."

On his seventeenth birthday, the 25th of August, 1861, the grandson of that King Louis of Bavaria who was the first among the princes of Germany to again take an active interest in the plastic arts, witnessed a performance of "Lohengrin," the first play that he had seen. Full of enthusiasm, he inquired for the other works of this master. Wagner's writings convinced him, who now had on his desk only the busts of Beethoven and Wagner, that the one seemed likely to meet the same fate that the other had in fact encountered—to sink into the grave before the attainment of his goal and of his fame. His silent vow was to reach out his hand to this "one" as soon as he should be king. Two years later, the "Ring of the Nibelungen" appeared in print. In it was the question: "Will this prince be found?" In the following spring the author of the work was in dire distress in Vienna. The silver rubles had rapidly disappeared. How could such common treasures be heeded by him who had at his disposal the Holy Grail? But inexorably approached the danger of loss of personal liberty. He had to fly. A friend had provided him a refuge on his estate in Switzerland. On the way there he remained a few days in Stuttgart. Of a sudden the friend's door-bell is rung, but Wagner's presence is denied. The stranger urges pressing business, and on inquiry informs the master of the house—who was none other than Carl Eckert, subsequently Hofkapellmeister at Berlin—that he comes in the name of the King of Bavaria! Louis II. by the sudden death of Maximilian II. had been called to the throne in March, 1864, and one of his first acts was the invitation extended to the artist, so enthusiastically admired.

"Now all has been won, my most daring hopes surpassed. He places all his means at my disposal," with these words he sank upon his friend's breast. In a short time he was in Munich.

"He has poured out his wealth upon me as from a horn of plenty," was the expression he used immediately after the first audience. "What shall I now tell you? The most inconceivable and yet the only thing I need has attained its full realization. In the year of the first representation of my 'Tannhaeuser,' a queen gave birth to the good genius of my life, who was destined to bring me out of deepest want into the highest happiness. He has been sent to me from heaven. Through him I am, and comprehend myself," he wrote, a few months later, after he had settled down in Munich, to a lady friend.

King Louis was a youth of true kingly form. In his beautiful eye there was at the same time a quiet enthusiasm. His keen understanding was accompanied by a lively imagination and a true soul, so that nature had endowed him with the three principal mental powers in noble proportions. His disposition is indicated by the words: "You are a Protestant? That is right. Always liberal." And after the style of youthful inexperience: "You likewise do not like women? They are so tedious." His soul and mind were open to the joyous reception of all ideal emotions. This was indeed a youthful king, as only such an artist could have wished, and permanently attracted. "To the Kingly Friend," is the title of the dedication of the "Walkuere," in the summer of 1864.

"O gracious king! protector of my life!
Thou fountain of all goodness, all delight;
Now, at the goal of my adventurous strife,
The words that shall express thy grace aright
I seek in vain, although the world is rife
With speech and printed book; and day and night
I still must seek for words to utter free
The gratitude my heart doth bear to thee."

Thereupon follow the three verses quoted above, and it comes to a close:

"So poor am I, I keep but only this—
The faith which thou hast given unto me;

It is the power by which to heights of bliss
My soul is lifted in proud ecstacy;
But partly is it mine, and I shall miss
Wholly its power, if thou ungracious be;
My gifts are all from thee, and I will praise
Thy royal faith that knows no change of days."

Of the latter there was to be no lack, although it was put to a severe test, and thus the artist reached at last the goal of his effort, referred to above, where he stands to-day, the artistic savior of his nation and his time.

As the main thing, the completion of the Nibelungen-Ring was taken in hand. In the meantime, however, a model exhibition of the new art-style was to be given, with "Tristan." For this purpose Schnorr was invited, at that time residing in Dresden. Wagner says, when he first met him at Carlsruhe, in 1862: "While the sight of the swan-knight, approaching in his little boat, gave me the somewhat odd impression of the appearance of a young Hercules (Schnorr suffered from obesity), yet his manner at once conveyed to me the distinct charm of the mythical hero sent by the gods, whose identity we do not study but whom we instinctively recognize. This instantaneous effect which touches the inmost heart, can only be compared to magic. I remember to have been similarly impressed in early youth by the great actress, Schroeder-Devrient, which shaped the course of my life, and since then not again so strongly as by Schnorr in Lohengrin." He had found in him a genuine singer, musician, and actor, possessing above all unbounded capacity for tragic roles.

He was put to the test at first in "Tannhaeuser," and in this new role he also produced an entirely new impression, of which the Munich public, led by Franz Lachner, in the worn-out tracks of the latter-day classics, had its first experience. Then followed the rehearsals for "Tristan," which Schnorr had already fully mastered, with the exception of a single passage, "Out of Laughter and Weeping, Joys and Wounds," the terrible love-curse in the third act. By his wonderful power of expression, the master had "made this clear to him." At the rehearsal of this act, Wagner staggered to his feet, profoundly moved, and embracing his wonderful friend, said softly that he could not express his joy over his now realized ideal, and Schnorr's dark eye flashed responsive pleasure. Buelow, who, as concert-master to the king, now resided in Munich, likewise conducted with wonderful precision the orchestra which Wagner himself had thoroughly rehearsed, and so the invitation was issued to this "art-festival" wherever Wagner's art had conquered hearts. It was to show how far the problem of original and genuine musico-dramatic art had been solved, and whether the people were ready for it and prepared to share in its grandest and noblest triumphs.

The public rehearsal was festive in its character. The whole musical press of Germany and some of the foreign critics were present. Wagner was called after every act. Unfortunately, the representation proper was delayed for nearly four weeks through the sickness of Frau Garrigues-Schnorr, who took the role of Isolde, so that the Munich people were after all the principal attendants. The applause was nevertheless enthusiastic, and the success of the memorable "art-festival" of June 10, 1865, admission to which was not to be had for money, but by invitation of Wagner and his royal friend, was an accomplished fact, notwithstanding the work had been by no means fully comprehended, for this required time. Unfortunately, the noble artist died a short time after, in Dresden, from the effects of a cold, to which the utter disregard of the theatre managers in Munich had exposed him in the scene where he had to lie wounded on a couch. Wagner was deeply affected. He conceived he had lost the solid stone work of his edifice, and would now have to resort to mere bricks. It is certain he never found a Siegfried as great as this Tristan.

Another contingency temporarily interfered with the undertaking of the two friends, and that was the opposition of the Munich public, which resulted in Wagner's permanent withdrawal from the city. To this public a person was indeed strange who made such unusual artistic demands, while the personal character and habits of Wagner at that time were probably nowhere more strange than in Bavaria, which had obtained its education at the hands of the Jesuit priests. It is true, the good qualities, such as simplicity of manners and habits of life, had remained, but the intellectual horizon had become a comparatively narrow one, and, what was worse, the clerical and aristocratic Bavarian party feared it would lose its power if a man like Wagner were to remain permanently about the king. George Herwegh has described comically enough the Witches-Sabbath, which that party, in 1865, with the aid of other hostile factions, enacted, and which forced Wagner once more into foreign lands.

Munich, accustomed to simplicity, took exception to the rich style in which Wagner furnished the villa presented by the king, and to the expansion of the civil-list for the construction of the theatre, which was to cost seven million marks, though it would have made Munich a festival-place for all Germany, and cultivated society the world over. The press from day to day printed some fresh calumny. It even assailed the private character of the artist after a fashion that provoked him to a very effective public defense. Even very sensible people became possessed, in an unaccountable manner, with the prevalent idea that Wagner was destroying Bavaria's prosperity. A not unknown author of oriental poetry, said ignorantly enough, that it was well such a tramp was finally to be driven off the street; and a college professor, who, it is true, had a son, a self-composer in Beethoven's meaning of the word, and who could therefore have performed all that Wagner did, added to this the brutal, insolent assertion, "the fellow deserves to be hanged." At last they prevailed upon the king, to whom this had been foolsplay, to listen at least to what unprejudiced men would tell him of public opinion in Bavaria. To the minister and the police-superintendent were added an esteemed ultra montane government counselor, an arch bishop and others who were reputed to be unprejudiced. His reply, "I will show to my dear people that I value their confidence and love above everything," proves that they finally succeeded in misleading even the greatest impartiality. The king himself requested the artist to leave Munich for some time and gave him an annuity of 15,000 marks. When this had been done, a public declaration of the principal party in Bavaria showed that the so-called "displeasure of the people" about political machinations and the like had been empty talk. Political, social, and artistic intrigues and base envy alone had given birth to this ghost.

This happened near the close of the year 1865. Wagner again turned to Switzerland. The king's affection for him had only been increased by these occurrences. He even visited his friend in his voluntary exile, who in turn had no more ardent desire than to meet such love with deeds, and calmly prepared himself again for new work. His longing for Munich had forever vanished. It is true, some of the nobler citizens sought to wipe out the disgrace with which the city had covered itself, by sending a silver wreath to Wagner on his birthday in 1866. The rejection of Semper's splendid design for the theatre by the civil-list led his thoughts anew to the wide German fatherland, and he at once returned to the Meistersingers, in the hope that by this more intelligible work the public would finally turn to him, and that then the great German people would assist in the erection of a festival-building for a national art-work and thus realize his grand ideal. We know to-day that he succeeded in uniting them in this great work.

The next important step in that direction was the representation of the "Meistersinger" in Munich in 1868. In the course of time Wagner dominated the stage in a manner which had not been witnessed since "Lohengrin."

It has been truthfully said that there was something more surprising than the highly poetic "Tristan," namely, the artist himself, who so shortly after could create a picture of such manifold coloring as the "Meistersinger." But with equal truth the same observer of Wagner says that whoever is astounded at this achievement has but little understood the one essential point in the nature and life of all really great Germans. "He does not know on what soil alone that many-sided humor displayed by Luther, Beethoven, and Wagner can grow, which other nations do not at all comprehend, and which even the Germans of to-day seem to have lost; that mixture, pure as gold, of simplicity, deep, loving insight, mental reflection and rollicking humor which Wagner has poured out like a delightful draught for all those who have keenly suffered in life, and who turn to him, as it were, with the smile of the convalescent." Another German, Sebastian Bach, might have been named whom Wagner resembles most in that universal dominating quality of mind which is even visible in the half-ironical, laughing eye of the simple Thuringian chorister, and brings home to us the truth of Faust's words, "creating delights for the gods to enjoy." He played at that time many of Bach's compositions, such as the "Well Tempered Clavicord," with his young assistant, Hans Richter, who had been recommended to him from Vienna as a copyist. What cared he for all this wild whirl of silly fancies and boorish conceit, so long as he, a genuine Prometheus, could create something new after the grandest models! In speaking of "Tannhaeuser" he tells us how supremely happy he was when occupied with the delightful work of real creation. "Before I undertake to write a verse or sketch a scene, I am already filled with the musical spirit of my creation," he writes in the year 1864. "All the characteristic motives are in my brain, so that when the text is done and the scenes arranged, the opera itself is completed, and the detailed musical treatment becomes rather a thoughtful and quiet after-work which the moment of actual composition has already preceded." The humor which at times prompted even the aged Beethoven to spring over tables and benches, frequently seized upon our master in such strange fashion that in the midst of company he would suddenly stand upon his head in a corner of the room for some time.

His friends observed with pleasure his rapturous happiness in the certainty of reaching the goal, even though it should bring him to the grave during this period of the "Meistersinger" composition. He lived in the most quiet retirement upon a small and beautiful estate in Triebscheu, near Lucerne, where Frau von Buelow, with her children, provided for his domestic comfort. His own wife had unexpectedly died a short time before. During her last years she had lived separately from the "fiery wheel" whose mad flight she could no longer grasp nor endure, but by no means in that poverty which the abominably slanderous press of Munich and elsewhere had accused him of inflicting upon her. On the contrary, she lived in circumstances fully corresponding to her husband's means.

In October, 1867, after the lapse of 22 years, the "Meistersinger" was at last completed. He now strove to secure as far as possible a model representation. It was of course to take place in Munich, where "Tristan" had already given the orchestra at least a sure tradition of style. The event was destined to win for him the very heart of the nation. If the general culture of the last generation by its shallow optimism and stale humanitarianism blunted the feeling for the tragic, as Wagner for the first time had deeply expressed it, yet of one quality we were never deprived, it ever remained undisturbed, and that was our German good-nature, from the depths of which humor springs. At a casual meeting in Kuxhasen, during a friendly contest in the expression of emotions by gestures of the face, even the great Kean could not rival the greater Devrient in one thing, and had to yield to him the victory, and that was the tearful smile which springs from real compassion with the sorrows of humanity. It was with this "German good-nature" that Wagner this time conquered the nations. It was Beethoven who had again quickened the flow from this deepest source of blessing in life which Shakespeare had been the first to fully open. By it, Wagner's soul has ever kept its warmth and spirit. Who that was present does not think with joyous emotion of those Munich May-days of 1868?

His pamphlet, "German Art and German Politics," had directed the attention of the narrower circle of Wagner's friends at least to the great fact that the artificial French civilization which had prevailed during the last generation could be banished by a real intellectual culture, and that in this work the highest form of art, the stage-festival-play, would take a prominent and important part. A masterly performance of Lohengrin in the spring of 1868, in honor of the Crown-Prince of Prussia, was a striking illustration of this, especially to Munich circles. It may also have influenced the mood of the performers in whose hands the ultimate realization of an object after all rests. "Even in after years Wagner confessed he had never felt greater satisfaction in his experiences with an opera company than at the first representation of the 'Meistersinger.'" The performers also speak of the persuasive grace and the fresh, animating cheerfulness with which the master, an example for all in his restless activity, moved among them and gave to each individual his constant directions. This remark of his biographer tells everything.

The rehearsals were this time even more artistically satisfactory to all the participants than those of "Tristan." This art-work was easier of comprehension owing to its more familiar subject and natural tone. At the director's desk stood Buelow—"a fine head with clear cut features, bold arched forehead and large eyes." Opposite to him on the stage stood Wagner, likewise a very active form of medium height. "All his features bear the impress of an unsubdued will which underlies his whole nature," says a Frenchman. "It shows itself everywhere—in the broad and prominent forehead, in the excessive curve of the strong chin, in the thin and compressed lips, up to the strong eyebrows, which disclose the long excitements of a life of suffering; it is the man of battle, whom we know by his life, the man of thought, who, never content with the past, looks constantly to the future." Closely attending, he accompanied every tone with a fitting gesture for the performer. Only when Mallinger sang the role of the goldsmith's little daughter, Eva, he paused and listened approvingly with a smiling face. It was clear that, like Prometheus among his lifeless forms, he animated them with the breath of the soul and roused them into life. Beckmesser, the Marker, by his drastic presentation alone expressed the full measure of furious wrath over the shoemaker's mockery of his beautiful singing. Such a display of art was new to all. The Court-Kapellmeister Esser of Vienna, admitted that for the first time he knew what dramatic, as compared with Kapellmeister-music, was; and the excellent clarinet-player Baermann, who had personally known Weber, felt himself in a new world, of which he said that one who did not know how to appreciate it was not worthy of it and that those who did not understand it were served rightly in being debarred from this enjoyment.

At the close of the rehearsals, Wagner expressed his great pleasure to all the performers; only the artist could again elevate art, and in contrast with the foreign style, hitherto cultivated, they would create our own distinctive art. The performance itself was intended to show to what height and dignity the drama could be elevated when earnest zeal and true loyalty are enlisted in its service. It was a touching proof of enthusiastic gratitude for the noble results to which he had led them, when they all gathered around him to press his hand or kiss his arms and shoulders. It was the first time that poet and artist were reunited and in harmony. A hopeful moment for our art! The enthusiasm lasted fully half of that fragrant summer night.

Such were the hopes realized by the happy impression the performance itself made upon everyone. The harmony of action, word, music, and scenery had hitherto never been consciously felt to such a degree. The rejoicing was general. The Sunday-afternoon service, so devout and home-like, the busy apprentices, the worthy masters, the "young Siegfried" Walther von Stolzing, the thoughtful, noble burgher form of Hans Sachs, and finally, lovely little Eva, no wonder it all produced supreme ecstasy. Wagner, sitting in the imperial box at the side of the king, cared not for the tumultous applause of those who had so grievously wronged him, but gave himself up to the enjoyment of this moment of the highest happiness, which perhaps was best reflected in the eyes of his noble friend. Finally, however, when the demand became too imperious, the king himself probably urged Wagner to go forward, and from the royal box he made his acknowledgment, too deeply stirred and agitated to utter a word. For the welfare of the nation and the time, we see here realized in its wide significance the vision of Schiller:

"Thus, King and Singer shall together be
Upon the mountains of humanity."

The friend of the cause will find a correct account of all these ever memorable occurrences in the "Musical Sketchbook—An Exposition of the State of the Opera at the present Time," of 1869, concerning which the master wrote to the author: "You will readily believe that much, indeed the most, of what you have written, has greatly affected and deeply touched me, and I shall therefore say nothing about your work itself except to express for all this my great and intense pleasure!"

The criticisms of different persons presented a many-colored picture of which an amusing sketch will also be found in the book referred to. How many Beckmessers came to light there! The most concise and worthiest expression of the prevalent feeling of final victory for the cause is found in the verses of Ernst Dohm, with which we close this grand chapter, the morning greeting of noble deeds:

No mistakes, no faults were found.
No,—but purely, lovely singing,
Captivating every heart,
Honor to the master bringing,
Glorifying German art—
Did the Mastersong resound.

Soon, as standard bearers strong,
From the strand of Isar, we
Will go forth with Mastersong
Through United Germany.

CHAPTER VI.

1869-1876.

BAIREUTH.

A Vienna Critic—"Judaism in Music"—The War of 1870—Wagner's Second Wife—"The Thought of Baireuth"—Wagner-Clubs—The "Kaiser March"—Baireuth—Increasing Progress—Concerts—The Corner-Stone of the new Theatre—The Inaugural Celebration—Lukewarmness of the Nation—The Preliminary Rehearsals—The Summer of 1876—Increasing Devotion of the Artists—The General Rehearsal—The Guests—The Memorable Event—Its Importance—A World-History in Art-Deeds.

"In the beginning was the deed."—GOETHE.

"As artist and man, I am now approaching a new world," Wagner had already written in 1851.

The Vienna Thersites, with his coarse and confused wits, whom the real irony of his time had termed "the most renowned musical critic of the age," had the hardihood to write for the principal newspaper of Austria as late as the spring of 1872: "Wagner is lucky in everything. He begins by raging against all monarchs, and a generous King meets him with enthusiastic love. Then he writes a pasquinade against the Jews, and musical Jewry pays him homage all the more by purchasing the Baireuth certificates. He proves that all our Hofkapellmeisters are mere artisans, and behold, they organize Wagner-clubs and recruit troops for Baireuth. Opera-singers and theatre directors, whose performances Wagner most cruelly condemns, follow his footsteps wherever he appears and are delighted if he salutes them. He brands our conservatories as being spoiled and neglected institutes, and the scholars of the Vienna conservatory form in line before Richard Wagner and make a subscription to present the master with a token of esteem."

Ah, yes; but this "luck" was the result of his close search for what was true and real.

This moral dignity, which asks for nothing but the truth, gradually drew toward Wagner many estimable friends, among them, through the "Meistersinger" performance in Munich, that simple citizen who organized in Mannheim the first of those Wagner-clubs that called into existence for us the high castle of art and the ideal—"Baireuth."

With that work Wagner had made the last hopeful attempt to improve the domestic stage. The experiences gained in this effort disclosed to him with distinct clearness the radically inartistic and un-German qualities of the theatre, which outwardly and inwardly, morally as well as spiritually, exerted an equally pernicious influence. But while completely alienating himself from it and planning only to "rear with considerate haste his gigantic edifice of four divisions," and thus obtain a stage free from all commercial interests, consecrated only to the ideal of the nation and the human mind, he yet felt impelled once more to withdraw with firm hand the veil from the actual social and art conditions of the nation, and wrote "Judaism in Music."

A simple pamphlet has rarely set all circles of society in such commotion as did this. It was like the awakening conscience of the nation, only that its mental stupor prevented the immediate comprehension of the new and deeply conciliatory spirit which here presented itself, at once to heal and to save. It was a national deed clearly to disclose this unseemly shopkeeper's spirit which attempts to drag to the mercantile level even the highest concerns of humanity. At the same time there came to some a conception of how deep and great, how overwhelming this German spirit must be, that it not only forces such aliens into its yoke, but, as in the case of Heine and Mendelssohn, often produces in them profoundly affecting tones of longing for participation in its sublime nature. Wagner's feeling at this, the most confused uproar which has been heard in the present time, could only have been like that of Goethe, namely, that all these stupid talkers have no idea how impregnable the fortress is in which he lives who is ever earnest about himself and his cause. He was unconcerned, knowing that he should have the privilege of performing his "Ring of the Nibelungen" far from all these distorted forms and figures of the prevailing art. Of this, his noble friend had given positive assurance; and for himself it became an unavoidable necessity, since in 1869 and 1870 Munich had performed, without his consent and contrary to his wishes, "Rheingold" and "Walkuere," by which it had only been shown anew how little the prevalent opera routine was in consonance with his object.

In the meantime came the war of 1870. That of 1866 had destroyed the rotten German "Bund," but now the most daring hopes revived in German breasts, for there stood the people in arms, like Lohengrin, everywhere repelling injustice and violence.

I dared to bury many a smart
Which long and deeply grieved my heart.

With these words Wagner greeted his king on the latter's birth day in 1870, and with clear-sighted boldness he said to himself, "The morning of mankind is dawning." The work, however, which was to glorify and render effective this first full Siegfried-deed of the Germans since the days of the Reformation, and revive the moral energy of the nation, was completed in June of the same year, 1870, with the "Goetterdaemmerung."

He now strove to strengthen himself anew and permanently. For the first time in his life he fully secured the purely human happiness which preserves our powers. He married the divorced Frau Cosima von Buelow, a daughter of Liszt. "This man, so completely controlled by his demon, should always have had at his side a high-minded, appreciative woman, a wife that would have understood the war that was constantly waged within him," is the judgment passed on Wagner's first wife by one of her friends. He had now found this woman, and in a way that proved on every hand a blessing. Her incomparably unselfish, self-sacrificing first husband himself declared afterwards that this was the only proper solution. Siegfried was the name given to the fruit of this union. The "Siegfried Idyl" of 1871 is dedicated to the boy's happy childhood in the beautiful surroundings of Lucerne.

In this year, the centennial anniversary of Beethoven's birth, he also told his nation what it possessed in him, its most manly son. He represents, as he says in that Jubilee pamphlet, the spirit so much feared beyond the mountains as well as on the other side of the Rhine. He regained for us the innocence of the soul. What is now wanting is, that out of this pure spirit-nature, as it is illustrated in his music, there shall arise a true culture in contrast with the foreign civilization, which resembles the time of the Roman emperors? These tones utter anew a world-saving prophesy, and shall we not then appropriate them fully and forever? The "thought of Baireuth" now obtained more definite form. A number of friends of the cause were to make it real and wrest German art from the Venusberg of the common theatre.

The work of the Wagner-clubs now began, which, with the aid of the Baireuth Board of Managers, under the direction of the indefatigable banker Fustel, has led to the goal at last. Liszt's Scholar, Tausig, and his friend, Frau von Schleinitz, in Berlin, organized the society of "Patrons," each member of which was to contribute one hundred thalers toward a fund of three hundred thousand. By the publication of his writings, Wagner himself introduced the cause that was to show that in his art also he sought that life by which the ideal nature of the nation exists. His noble-minded king had, in November of 1870, uttered the words of deliverance to the other German princes, which finally gave us again a dignified and honorable existence as a nation, by creating the German empire. Could German art then remain in the background? Our artist was now all activity—a wonderfully joyous and stirring activity. To the "German army before Paris," he who had always thought and labored for his nation's glory, sang, in January, 1871, the song of triumphant joy of the German armies' deeds:

The Emperor comes: let justice now in peace have sway.

At that time, also, he composed, at the suggestion of Dr. Abrahams, owner of the "Peters edition," in Leipzig, the Kaiser March, which closes with the following people's song:

God save the Emperor, William, the King!
Shield of all Germans, freedom's defense!
The highest crown
Graces thine head with renown!
Peace, won with glory, be thy recompense!
As foliage new upon the oak-tree grows,
Through thee the German Empire new-born rose;
Hail to its ancient banners which we
Did carry, which guided thee
When conquering bravely the Gallic foes!
Defying enemies, protecting friends,
The welfare of the nations Germany defends.

Shortly afterward he expresses more clearly the meaning of the festival-plays that are to be representations in a nobler and original German style, and he, the lonely wanderer, who hitherto has heard but the croakings in the bogs of theatrical criticism, accompanied the pamphlet with an essay on the "Mission of the Opera," with which he at the same time introduces himself as a member of the Berlin Academy.

In the spring of 1871, he went to Baireuth, the ancient residence of the Margraves, which contained one of the largest theatres. The building was arranged for the wants of the court and not fully adapted to his purposes, but the simple and true-hearted inhabitants of the place had attracted him. Besides this, the pleasant, quiet little city was situated in the "Kingdom of Grace" and, what likewise seemed of importance, in the geographical centre of Germany. A short stay subsequently in the capital of the new empire revealed his goal at once with stronger consciousness and purpose both for himself and his friends. At a celebration held there in his honor he said that the German mind bears the same relation to music as to religion. It demands the truth and not beautiful form alone. As the Reformation had laid the foundations of the religion of the Germans deeper and stronger by freeing Christianity from Roman bonds, so music must retain its German characteristics of profoundness and sublimity. During the same time the building of the theatre after Semper's designs was planned with the building inspector, Neumann.

The sudden death of Tausig which occurred at this time seemed a heavy loss to all. Wagner has erected for him an inspiring and touching monument in verse. Other friends however came forward all the more actively, particularly from Mannheim, with its music-dealer, Emil Heckel, who had asked him what those without means could do for the great cause and then at once commenced to organize the "Richard Wagner-Verein." The example was immediately followed by Vienna and the other German cities. The project was so far advanced that negotiations with Baireuth could now be opened. The city was found willing enough to provide a building site. Applications of other cities having in view their material interests could therefore be ignored. Wagner then in order to clearly state the definite purpose to be accomplished, published the "Report to the German Wagner-Verein," which reveals to us so deeply the soul-processes that were connected with the completion of his stage-festival-play. "I have now to my intense pleasure only to unite the propitious elements under the same banner which floats so auspiciously over the resurrected German empire, and at once I can build up my structure out of the constituent parts of a real German culture; nay more, I need only to unveil the prepared edifice, so long unrecognized, by withdrawing from it the false drapery which will soon like a perforated veil disappear in the air." Thus he closes with joyous hope. And now the necessary steps were taken in Baireuth. The city donated the building site. The laying of the corner-stone of the temporary building was to be celebrated May 22, 1872, with Beethoven's Ninth symphony. Wagner took up his permanent residence in Baireuth. The King had sent his secretary to meet him while en-route through Augsburg and to assure him that whatever the outcome might be he would be responsible for any deficit.

A paragraph in the prospectus of the Mannheim society had held out the prospect of concerts under the master's own direction. This led to a number of journeys that gave him an opportunity to make the acquaintance of his "friends" and especially of the artistic "forces" of Germany. The first journey, as was proper, was to Mannheim "where men are at home." They had there, as he said, strengthened his faith in the realization of his plans and demonstrated that the artist's real ground was in the heart of the nation! Thus he interpreted the meaning of the celebration there. Vienna also heard classical music, as well as his own, under the direction of his magical baton. It happened that at "Wotan's Departure," and "the Banishment of the fire-god, Loge," in the "Walkuere," a tremendous thunder-storm broke forth. "When the Greeks contemplated a great work, they called upon Zeus to send them a flash of lightning as an omen. May all of us who have united to found a home for German art interpret this lightning also as favorable to our work, and as a sign of approval from above," he said amidst indescribable sensation, and then touched upon the Baireuth festival, and the Ninth symphony, in which the German soul appears so deep and rich in meaning. What a world of thoughts, what germs of future forms lie concealed in this symphony! He himself stands upon this great work, and from this vantage strives to advance further. During this period the ill-omened raven, Professor Hanslick, uttered his silly words about Wagner's "luck." But the victory was this time with the right.

In Baireuth meanwhile all was being prepared for the celebration. The Riedel and the Rebling singing-societies constituted the nucleus of the chorus while the orchestra was formed of musicians from all parts of Germany, Wilhelmi at their head. There the master for the first time was really among "his artists." "We give no concert, we make music for ourselves and desire simply to show the world how Beethoven is performed—the devil take him who criticises us," he said to them with humorous seriousness. The laying of the corner-stone on the beautiful hill overlooking the city, where the edifice stands to-day, took place May 22, 1872, to the strains of the "Huldigungs March," composed for his King in 1864. "Blessing upon thee, my stone, stand long and firm!" were the words with which Wagner himself gave the first three blows with the hammer. The King had sent a telegram: "From my inmost soul, I convey to you, my dearest friend, on this day so important for all Germany, my warmest and sincerest congratulations. May the great undertaking prosper and be blessed! I am to-day more than ever united with you in spirit." Wagner himself had written the verse:

Here I enclose a mystery;
For centuries it here may rest.
So long as here preserved it be,
It shall to all be manifest.

Both telegram and verse with the Mannheim and Bayreuth documents lie beneath the stone. Wagner returned with his friends to the city in a deeply earnest mood. On this his sixtieth birthday his eyes for the first time beheld the goal of his life!

At the celebration, which then took place in the Opera-house, he addressed the following words to his friends and patrons: "It is the nature of the German mind to build from within. The eternal God actually dwells therein before the temple is erected to His glory. The stone has already been placed which is to bear the proud edifice, whenever the German people for their own honor shall desire to enter into possession with you. Thus then may it be consecrated through your love, your good wishes and the deep obligation which I bear to you, all of you who have encouraged, helped and given to me! May it be consecrated by the German spirit which away over the centuries sends forth its youthful morning-greeting to you."

The performance of the symphony of that artist, to whom Wagner himself attributes religious consecration according to eye-witnesses, gave to this festival, also "the character of a sacred celebration," as had once been true of the great Beethoven academy in November, 1814. At the evening celebration, however, Wagner recalled again the large-heartedness of his King, and said that to this was due what they had experienced to-day, but that its influence reached far beyond civil and state affairs. It guaranteed the ultimate possession of a high intellectual culture, and was the stepping-stone to the grandest that a nation can achieve. Would the time soon come which shall fitly name this King, as it already recognized him, a "Louis the German" in a far nobler sense than his great ancestor? "Certainly no fear of the always existing majority of the vulgar and the coarse is to prevent us from confessing that the greatest, weightiest and most important revelation which the world can show is not the world-conqueror but he who has overcome the world:" thus teaches the philosopher, and we shall soon perceive that this was also true of Wagner and his royal friend.

The fame of this celebration, which had so deeply stirred everyone present, resounded through all countries, appealed to all true German hearts. And yet, how many remained even now indifferent and incredulous! The "nation," as such, did not respond to the call. It did not, or would not, understand it, uttered by a man who had told us so many unwelcome truths to our face. It still lay paralyzed in foreign and unworthy bondage, and was, besides, for the time too much engrossed with the affairs of the empire, whose novelty had not yet worn off.

"From morn till eve, in toil and anguish,
Not easily gained it was."

These words of *Wotan*, about his castle Walhalla, were only to be too fully realized by our master. His "friends" alone gave him comfort, and their number he saw constantly increase from out of the midst of the people whose leaders in art-matters they were more and more destined to become. The public interest was kept alive and stirred afresh with concerts and discourses. The Old did not rest. The struggle constantly broke out anew, and for the time it remained in the possession of the ring that symbolizes mastery. The dragon was still unconquered. As the "people" in Germany are not particularly wealthy, slow progress was made with the contributions from the multiplying Wagner-clubs, and yet millions were needed even for this temporary edifice with its complete stage apparatus. It required all the love of his friends, especially of that rarest of all friends, to dispel at times his deep anger when he was compelled to see how mediocrity, even actual vulgarity, again and again held captive the minds of his people to whom he had such high and noble things to offer. "In the end I must accept the money of the Jews in order to build a theatre for the Germans," he said, in the spring of 1873, to Liszt, when during that period of wild stock-speculations, some Vienna bankers had offered him three millions of marks for the erection of his building. He could not well have been humiliated more deeply before his own people, but he was raised still higher in the consciousness of his mission. Truly, this love also came "out of laughter and tears, joys and sorrows," for the mighty host of his enemies now put forth every effort to make his work appear ridiculous and in that way kill it. A pamphlet, by a physician, declared him "mentally diseased by illusions of greatness." Even a Breughel could not paint the raging of the distorted figures which at that time convulsed the world of culture, not alone of Germany. It was really an inhuman and superhuman struggle around this ring of the Nibelung!

Nevertheless, in August of the same year (1873), the festival could be undertaken in Baireuth. "Designed in reliance upon the German soul, and completed to the glory of its august benefactor," is printed on the score of the Nibelungen Ring, which now began to appear. The space for the "stage-festival-play" was at least under roof. But with that, the means obtained so far were exhausted, and only "vigorous assistance" on the part of his King prevented complete cessation of work. Wagner himself was soon compelled again to take up his wanderer's staff. He sought this time (1874-1875), with the lately completed "Goetterdaemmerung," to sound through the nation the effective call to awaken, and in doing so met with many decided encouragements. "From the bottom of my heart I thank the splendid Vienna public which to-day has brought me an important step nearer the realization of my life-mission." This was the theme which fortunately he had then only to vary in Pesth and in Berlin.

The preliminary rehearsals now began, and what Munich had witnessed in 1868 repeated itself ten times over in Baireuth during this summer of 1875. For weeks there was the same untiring industry, but also the same, nay increasing, enthusiasm. "Of this marvelous work I recently heard more than twenty rehearsals. It over-tops and dominates our entire art-period as does Mont Blanc the other mountains," wrote Liszt. The master frankly conceded that it was due to the "unhesitating zeal of the associate artists as well as to the splendid success of their performances" that he could now positively invite the patrons and Wagner for the next summer. "Through your kind participation may an artistic deed be brought to light, such as none of the dignitaries of to-day but only the free union of those really called could present to the world," he says. And:

"From such marvelous deed the hero's fame arose,"

sings Hagen of Siegfried.

The rehearsals during the summer of 1876 so increased the enthusiastic devotion of the artists to the work, that many felt they had really now only become such. Others, however, like Niemann as Siegmund, Hill as Alberich, and Schlosser as Mime, showed already in fact what heroic deeds in the art of representation were presented. The fetters of the maidenly bride were indeed broken that she might live. "We have overcome the first. We must yet consummate a true hero-deed in a short time," Wagner said, when at the first close of the Cycle silent emotion had given place to a perfect storm of enthusiasm, but, he exultantly added: "If we shall carry it out as I now clearly see that it will be done, we may well say that we have performed something grand." The little anticipated humor in "Siegfried" developed itself in such a way under the leadership of Hans Richter, who was more and more inspired by the master, that one seemed indeed to hear "the laughter of the universe in one stupendous outbreak." That was the fruit of the "tempestuous sobbing" with which young Siegfried himself had once listened to the Ninth symphony. It was indeed a new soul-foundation for his nation and his time! Wagner himself calls an enthusiasm of this kind a power that could conduct all human affairs to certain prosperity and upon which states could be built. The patriotic enthusiasm of 1870 sprang from the same source and it has brought us the "empire" as that of 1876 gave us the "art."

The general rehearsal on the seventh of August was attended by the King. He had stopped at a sub-station, once the favorite resort of Jean Paul, and at the station-master's house the two great and constant friends silently embraced, giving vent to their feelings in tears. From that date to the thirteenth of August, 1876, the ever memorable day of the re-creation of German art, came the hosts of friends and patrons, from great princes to the humble German musicians. "Baireuth is Germany" is the acclamation of an Englishman on witnessing the spectacle. The head of the realm, Emperor William, was there himself welcomed by the festival-giver and hailed with acclamation by the thousands from far and near. The Grand-duke Constantine and the Emperor of Brazil were likewise present.

Of the effect we shall at this time say nothing for lack of space to tell all; but, to convey at least a conception of the event which riveted minds and held hearts spell-bound until the last note had passed away, while at the same time a whole new world dawned upon our souls—we present a short account of the work as pithily drawn by Wagner's gifted friend and patron, Prof. Nietzsche, in Basle.

"In the Ring of the Nibelungen," he says, "the tragic hero is a god (Wotan), who covets power and who, by following every path to obtain it, binds himself with contracts, loses his liberty and is at last engulfed in the curse which rests upon power. He becomes conscious of his loss of liberty, because he no longer has the means to gain possession of the golden ring, the essence or symbol of all earthly power, and at the same time of greatest danger for himself as long as it remains in the hands of his enemies. The fear of the end and the 'twilight' of all the gods comes over him and likewise despair, as he realizes that he can not strive against this end, but must quietly see it approach. He stands in need of the free, fearless man, who without his advice and aid, even battling against divine order, from within himself accomplishes the deed which is denied to the gods. He does not discover him, and just as a new hope awakens he must yield to the destiny that binds him. Through his hand the dearest must be destroyed, the purest sympathy punished with his distress.

"Then at last he loathes the power that enslaves and brings forth evil. His will is broken, and he desires the end which threatens from afar. And now what he had but just desired occurs. The free, fearless man appears. He is created supernaturally, and they who gave birth to him pay the penalty of a union contrary to nature. They are destroyed, but Siegfried lives.

"In the sight of his splendid growth and development the loathing vanishes from the soul of Wotan. He follows the hero's fate with the eye of the most fatherly love and anxiety. How Siegfried forges the sword, kills the dragon, secures the ring, escapes the most crafty intrigues, and awakens Brunhilde; how the curse that rests upon the ring does not spare even him, the innocent one, but comes nearer and nearer; how he, faithful in faithlessness, wounds out of love the most beloved, and is surrounded by the shadows and mists of guilt, but at last emerges as clear as the sun and sinks, illuminating the heavens with his fiery splendor and purifying the world from the curse—all this the god, whose governing spear has been broken in the struggle with the freest and who has lost his power to him, holds full of joy at his own defeat, fully participating in the joy and sorrow of his conqueror. His eye rests with the brightness of a painful serenity upon all that has passed. 'He has become free in Love, free from himself.'"

These are the profound contents of a work that reveals to us the tragic nature of the world!

At the close of the Cycle, there arose in the enthusiastic assemblage a demand to see at such a great and grand moment the noble artist whose eyes had rested for so many years upon the spirit of his great nation "with the brightness of a painful serenity." He could not evade the persistent, stormy demand, and had to appear. His features bore an expression that seemed to show a whole life lived again, an entire world embraced anew, as he came forward and uttered the significant yet simple words: "To your own kindness and the ceaseless efforts of my associates, our artists, you owe this accomplishment. What I have yet to say to you can be put into a few words, into an axiom. You have seen now what we can do. It remains for you to will! And if you will, then we have a German art!"

Yes, indeed we have such an art—a "Baireuth."

O, done is the deathless deed;
On mountain-top the mighty castle!
Splendidly shines the structure new.
As in dreams I did dream it,
As my will did wish it,
Strong and serene it stands to the view—
Mighty manor new!

We have a German art! But have we also by this time a German spirit that sways the nation's life? Have we come to detest mere might which we have hitherto worshipped and that yet "bears within its lap evil and thralldom?" Has the "free, fearless man," the Siegfried, been born to us who out of himself creates the right and with the sword he forges manfully slays the dragon that gnaws at the vitals of our being and thus rescues the slumbering bride? This question has been hurled into our life and history by the "Ring of the Nibelungen." It will be heard as long as the question remains unsolved. If, according to Wagner's conception, Beethoven wrote the history of the world in music, then he himself has furnished a world-history in art-deeds! Such is the meaning of this Baireuth with its Nibelungen Ring of 1876.

Let us see now what the life and work of this artist, for nigh unto seventy years, further and finally imports to us. He also was guided by Goethe's fervent prayer:

"O, lofty Spirit, suffer me
The end of my life's-work to see!"

CHAPTER VII.

1877-1882.

PARSIFAL.

A German Art—Efforts to maintain the Acquired Results—Concerts in London—Recognition abroad and Lukewarmness at home—The "Nibelungen" in Vienna—"Parsifal"—Increasing Popularity of Wagner's Music—Judgments—Accounts of the "Parsifal" Representations—The Theatre Building—"Parsifal," a National Drama—Its Significance and Idea—Anti-Semiticism—The Jewish Spirit—Wagner's Standpoint—Synopsis of "Parsifal"—The Legend of the Holy Grail—Its Symbolic Importance—Art in the Service of Religion—Beethoven and Wagner—"Redemption to the Redeemer."

"Dawn then now, thou day of Gods!"—Wagner.

"If you but will it, we shall have a German art." It is true we had a German music, a German literature, a German art of painting, each of high excellence, but they were not that union of German art which floated before Wagner's mind in his "combined art-work" and which found its first adequate interpretation in the performances of the Nibelungen Ring. His object was now to make it permanent and to this end he sought the means.

Accordingly on January 1, 1877, the invitation to form "a society of patrons for the culture and maintenance of the stage-festival-plays of Baireuth" was issued. At the same time the "Baireuther Blaetter," which subsequently were made available to the general public, were issued in order to more fully and constantly elucidate the aim and object of the cause. Wagner had declined to acquiesce in a demand for a subsidy from the Reichstag, although King Louis had agreed to support such a measure before the Bundesrath. "There are no Germans; at least they are no longer a nation. Whoever still thinks so and relies upon their national pride makes a fool of himself," he said bitterly enough to a friend. As far as the ideal is concerned he was certainly right in regard to the Reichstag as well as the people. "He who can clear such paths is a genius, a prophet, and in Germany, a martyr as well!" are the words of one of those who at one time had contemptuously spoken of this "Baireuth" as a "speculation." And yet Wagner had to accept an invitation to give concerts in London to cover the expenses of this same "Baireuth." By the distinguished reception the artist met there, the consideration shown for his art, the spread of his earlier works over the whole of Europe, he felt that foreign lands had understood him, the German. It must have been very bitter for him to feel that the Germans as a nation knew him not. Among the multitude of the educated, faith was still wanting. They courted foreign gods. If it had not been so would it have required seven, fully seven years, to obtain the moderate sum needed even to think of resuming the work, and in the end a contribution of three hundred thousand marks from His Majesty the King to bring it to completion? How slow was the progress of the society of patrons! People who, during the era of speculation had accumulated wealth rapidly, thought in these years of decreasing prosperity of something else than joining such an undertaking, and declared that they had to economize. And yet the annual dues were but 15 marks! Very singular was the answer of some whose rank or learning gave them prominence. They said that it was not even known whether the project had any real standing and they might therefore disgrace themselves by lending their names. Yes, when the bad Wagnerians dared to attack the tottering Mendelssohn-Schuman instrumental mechanics, Germans as well as others were induced to withdraw from the society which it had cost them so much struggle to join. Councilors of State and educators did not even respond to the invitations of the society's branches which were now gradually organized in a large number of cities.

It was generally known that a new work was soon to issue from Wagner's brain and soon everywhere from the Rhine to the Danube, from rock to sea, could be heard the Nibelungen! Wagner had, against his innermost conviction, consented to permit the use of the work by the larger theatres in the supposition that such personal experience of the "prodigious deed" would open heart and hand for a still grander one, the permanent establishment of a distinctive German art. Vienna came first. However excellent the performance of a few, for instance, Scaria as Wotan, Materna as Brunnhilde and the orchestra under Hans Richter, there was lacking the ensemble! The sensation of something extraordinary, of grandeur and solemnity, that in Baireuth had elevated the soul to the eternal heights of humanity, was not there. It was often as when daylight enters a theatre; the sublime illusion of such a tragic representation was wanting, and Wagner knew that in this art it is the very bread of life. "The art-work also, like everything transitory, is only a parable, but a parable of the ever-present eternal," he said, in taking leave of his friends and patrons in Baireuth and his purpose now was deeply to impress the minds of his contemporaries with this "ever-present eternal" and thus make it permanently effective. The Holy Grail had first to give forth its last wonder!

Once more he diverts his attention from "outward politics," as he called the intercourse with the theatres, and collects his thoughts for a new deed. This was "Parsifal." With this work, performed for the first time, July 26,

1882, and then repeated thirteen times, he believed he might close his life-long labors, and assuredly he has securely crowned them. It seems indeed as if this has finally and forever broken the obstinate ban that so long separated him and his art from his people. The success of the Nibelungen Ring had been called in question, but that of "Parsifal" is beyond doubt, as sufficiently demonstrated by the attendance of cultured people from everywhere for so many weeks! "They came from all parts of the world; as of old in Babel, you can hear speech in every tongue," said a participant in the festival. With the final slaying of the dragon, there fell also into the hero's hand the treasure, inasmuch as the large attendance left a surplus of many thousand marks, thus assuring the continuation of the festival-plays.

To be sure, the Nibelungen Ring had largely contributed to this success. At first performed in Leipzig, then by the same troupe in Berlin, it had met with a really unprecedented reception. Since the storm of 1813, since the years of 1848-49, the feeling of a distinctive nationality has not been so effectually roused, and this time it no longer stood solely upon the ground of patriotism and politics, but there where we seek our highest—the "ever-present eternal." England was likewise roused in 1882, with performances of the "Nibelungen Ring," and still more with "Tristan," to a consciousness of an eternal humanity in this art, such as had not been experienced there since Beethoven's Ninth symphony, and this enthusiasm of our manly and serious brethren sped like the fire's glare, illuminating the common fatherland from whence they had themselves once carried that feeling for the tragic which produced their Shakespeare. Everywhere was the stir of spring-time, sudden awakening, as from death-like slumber or a disturbing dream. "Dawn then now, thou day of gods!"

We will next give some accounts of the representations.

"'Victory! Victory!' is the word which is making the rounds of the world from Baireuth, in these days. Wagner's latest creation which brings the circle of his works in a beautiful climax to a dignified close, has achieved a success such as the most intimate adherents of the master could not well desire fuller or grander. The name of a 'German Olympia,' which had been given facetiously to the capital of Upper Franconia, it really now merited," was said by a London correspondent.

At the close of the general rehearsal, "the participating artists unanimously declared that they had never received from the stage such an impression of lofty sublimity." "Parsifal produces such an enormous effect that I can not conceive any one will leave the theatre unsatisfied or with hostile thoughts," E. Heckel wrote; and Liszt affirmed that nothing could be said about this wonderful work: "Yes, indeed, it silences all who have been profoundly touched by it. Its sanctified pendulum swings from the lofty to the most sublime." Of the first act it had already been said: "We here meet with a harmony of the musico-dramatic and religious church style which alone enables us to experience in succession the most terrible, heartrending sorrow and again that most sanctified devotion which the feeling of a certainty of salvation alone rouses in us."

The German Crown-Prince attended the performance of August 29th, the last one. "I find no words to voice the impression I have received," he said to the committee of the patron society which escorted him. "It transcends everything that I had expected, it is magnificent. I am deeply touched, and I perceive that the work can not be given in the modern theatre." And, finally, "I do not feel as though I am in a theatre, it is so sublime."

A Frenchman wrote: "The work that actually created a furious storm of applause is of the calmest character that can be conceived; always powerful, it leaves the all-controlling sensation of loftiness and purity." "The union of decoration, poetry, music and dramatic representation in a wonderfully beautiful picture, that with impressive eloquence points to the new testament—a picture full of peace and mild, conciliatory harmony, is something entirely new in the dramatic world," is said of the opening of the third act.

And in simple but candid truth the decisive importance of the cause called forth the following: "Parsifal furnishes sufficient evidence that the stage is not only not unworthy to portray the grandest and holiest treasures of man and his divine worship, but that it is precisely the medium which is capable in the highest degree of awakening these feelings of devotion and presenting the impressive ceremony of divine worship. If the hearer is not prompted to devotion by it, then certainly no church ceremony can rouse such a feeling in him. The stage, that to the multitude is at all times merely a place of amusement, and upon which at best are usually represented only the serious phases of human life, of guilt and atonement, but which is deemed unworthy of portraying the innermost life of man and his intercourse with his God, this stage has been consecrated to its highest mission by 'Parsifal.'"

The building also, which Semper's art-genius, with the highest end in view had constructed, is worthy of this mission. It has no ornament in the style of our modern theatres. Nowhere do we behold gold or dazzling colors; nowhere brilliancy of light or splendor of any kind. The seats rise amphitheatrically and are symmetrically enclosed by a row of boxes. To the right and left rise mighty Corinthian columns, which invest the house with the character of a temple. The orchestra, like the choir of the Catholic cloisters, is invisible and everything unpleasant and disturbing about ordinary theaters is removed. Everything is arranged for a solemn, festive effect. "That is no longer the theatre, it is divine worship," was the final verdict accordingly. "Baireuth" is the temple of the Holy Grail.

At length we come to the principal theme, and with it to the climax of this historical sketch of such a mighty and all-important artistic lifework, to "Parsifal" itself. The mere mention of its contents attests its importance for the present and the future. Wagner's "Parsifal," in an important sense, can be termed our national drama. Such a work like Æschylus' "Persian" and Sophocles' Oedipus-trilogy, should recall to the consciousness of a world-historical people the period in which it stands in the world's history, and thereby make clear the mission it has to fulfil.

That we Germans have begun again to make world-history in a political sense, since the last generation, is evidenced by the great action of the time which seems for the present to have settled the politics of Europe and extended its influence upon the world at large. Beyond the domain of politics however the real movers of the world are the ideas which animate humanity and of which politics are but a sign of life possessing subordinate influence. In this movement of the mind we Germans are, without question, much older than a mere generation, as indeed Wagner's poetic material everywhere confirms. The one work in which Kaulbach's genius triumphed, the "Battle of the Huns," gained for him a world-wide fame, more by the plastic idea revealed in the perpetual struggle of the spirits than by its artistic execution. We stand to-day before, or rather in, a like mighty contest. Two moral religious sentiments struggle against each other for life and death in invisible as well as visible conflict. To which shall be the victory?

In the year 1850 Wagner wrote a pamphlet of weighty import. It reveals an expression of the utmost moment, though it has been heeded least by those whom it concerns as much as life and death; or, rather, it has not been understood at all, because these natures are more attracted by the trivial. Its most impressive confirmation is to-day furnished by art, above all else by actual representations on the boards that typify the world. "Parsifal" also is such a symbol, and in so large a world-historical and even metaphysical sense, that by it the stage has become a place dedicated to the proclamation of highest truth and morality. We have seen the grotesque anti-Semitic movement and the lamentable persecution of the Jews. What could inflict more injury to our higher nature, to our real culture? And yet in this lies concealed a deep instinct of a purely moral nature. It does not, however, concern merely that people whom the course of events has cast among other nations, still much less the individual man, who, without choice or intention, has been born among, and therefore forms a part of them. It involves the secret of the world-historical problems that struggle so long with each other until the right one triumphs. To these problems, with his incomparable depth of soul, the whole life and work of our artist is devoted as long as he breathes and lives, moved by the holiest feeling for his nation, for the time—yes, for mankind, in whose service he as real "poet and prophet" stands with every fibre of his nature and works with every beat of his heart.

That unnoticed, misunderstood expression at the close of the paper by "K. Freigedank," in 1850, was this: "One more Jew we must name, who appeared among us as a writer, namely, Boerne. He stepped out of his individual position as Jew, seeking deliverance among us. He did not find it, and must have become conscious that he would only find it in our own transformation also into genuine men. To return in common with us to a purer humanity, however, signifies, for the Jew, above all else, that he shall cease to be a Jew. Boerne had fulfilled this. But it was precisely Boerne who taught us how this deliverance cannot be achieved in cool comfort and listless ease; but that it involves for them, as for us, toil, distress, anxiety, and abundance of pain and sorrow. Strive for this by self-abandonment and the regenerating work of salvation, and then we are united and without difference! But, remember that your deliverance depends upon the deliverance of Ahasrer—his destruction!"

No other people has received those cast out by all the world with such sacredly pure, humane feeling as the Germans. Will they then at last find their deliverance among us from the curse of homelessness, their new existence by absorption into a larger, richer, deeper whole? It is this question which animates and moves Wagner; but by no means in the sense of a casual and shifting quarrel among different races or even religious parties. On the contrary, he feels that this question is a life-question of the time, approaching its final solution. It is not the Jews, however, but the Jewish spirit, that represents the antagonist—that spirit which at first, after the birth of Christianity, and aided by the filth of Roman civilization, with its inherent evil germs, this people devoted to a world-historic power of evil; and which, even in its most brilliant revelation, in Spinoza, as has been most clearly demonstrated from his own works by Schopenhauer, seeks only its own advantage, to which it sacrifices the whole, but does not recognize the whole to which it must lovingly sacrifice itself.

Such concrete, actual historical developments Wagner regards not as a hindrance, but as the external support of his art-work. For a poetic composition requires some connection with a time or space to make perceptible to the senses its view of the advancing development of the mind of humanity. So it is that Kleist's "Arminius-battle" does not in the least refer to the ancient Romans, but to the degenerate race, the mixture of tiger and ape, as Voltaire has called them, and in this symbol of art he strengthened the determination of his people until in the battles of nations it conquered. Wagner even transfers the scene of this conflict into those distant centuries in which the struggle between Christians and Infidels was very fierce, while that between Jews and Occidentals had not yet even in existence. Like the real artist, he also uses only individual phases of the present time, which, it is quite true, bear but too close a relation to the character of that Arabian world that once engaged in conflict with Christianity for the world's control, and thus proves that this question, least of all is a passing "Question of time and controversy," but is one of the ever-present questions of humanity which has again come to the front in a specially vivid and urgent form. His inborn feeling for the purely human, which we have seen displayed with such touching warmth in all his doings, and that has created for us the genuine human forms of a "Flying Dutchman," "Tannhaeuser," "Lohengrin," and "Siegfried" is true to itself this time, indeed this time more than ever. He anticipates the struggling aspiration. He sees the form already appear on the surface, and only seeks a pure human sympathy to show the true and full solution which denies to neither of the disputing parties the God-given right of existence.

Klingsor, the sorcerer, representative of everything hostile to the Holy Grail and its knights, summons Kundry, the maid, subject to his witchcraft—in other words to that evil moral law which the individual alone is unable to resist—and reproachfully says:

Shame! that with the brood of knights,
Thou should'st like a beast be maintained!

The German class-pride which regarded the Jew as a body servant is strongly enough characterized and our own ancient injustice still more sharply expressed in his words:

"Thus may the whole body of knights
In deadly conflict each other destroy."

Thus Wagner reveals still more clearly than in the "Flying Dutchman" with his "fabulous homesickness" an absolute trait and the inner view of that sentiment which here longs for salvation, to be mortal with the mortals. At the sight of the nobler qualities and real human dignity which Kundry for the first time in her life sees in the person of Parsifal, who has been born again through the recognition of the truth, she breaks down completely and with the only word that she now knows, "serve! serve!" she throws all evil selfishness away. For the first time it is now fully disclosed how deeply after all, and with what intensity those of alien race and religion serve the ideas, not so much of our own similarly narrow contracted race-life, but those ideas which have transformed us from a mere nation to an historical part of humanity that guards the world's eternal treasure in this Holy Grail, as its last and grandest possession.

How fully is Goethe's saying "the power that ever seeks the evil and yet produces good" realized. Kundry is the messenger of the same Holy Grail against which her lord and master conducts the fatal war. To all distant lands it is she that brings the higher element of culture, the purer humanity which she gets from the Grail and its life. Though the peculiar portraiture of Kundry is drawn from his own experience of the present, the poet has gone still further and pictured that omnipresent spirit of evil which can never by simple participation in the sorrows of others gain knowledge of the perpetual sorrow of the world. Klingsor summons from the chaotic, primeval foundation of the world, where good and evil still lie commingled, the blind instinct of nature, as that wonderful element in the world's history which must everywhere be at once servant of the devil and messenger of grace, with the all-comprehensive words:

"Thy master calls thee, nameless one;
Primeval devil! rose of hell!
Herodias thou wast and what more?
Gundryggia there, Kundry here!"

It is the feminine Ahasrer, present in all ages and spheres, in our time revealing its tangible form in the ruling spirit of Judaism. As her sinful nature at last is overcome by Parsifal's purity, and she humbly approaches him to receive the baptism that is awarded to every one who believes and acts in the spirit of pure humanity, he proclaims, when he has withstood her temptation and thereby has regained from Klingsor the holy lance of the Grail, the impending catastrophe by tracing with the lance the sign of the cross and saying:

"With this sign thy spell I banish!
Even as it heals the wound
Which with it thou hast dealt—
So may thy delusive splendor in grief and ruin fall."

When in the last century, Roman Catholicism had become sensual and worldly through Jesuitism, and Protestantism had put on either the straight-jacket of orthodoxy or had been diluted with rationalism, there came to the surface, outside of the religious sects, secret societies, such as the Freemasons. In their well-meant but flat humanitarian idealism, those strangers to our race and religion, the hitherto despised Jews, also took active part and what "delusive splendor" have they not since then provided for themselves in literature and art and general ways of life? A single actual resurrection of that sign in which we Germans alone have attained world-culture and world-importance has "in grief and ruin destroyed" all this, and we hope in truth that we are now approaching a new epoch of our spiritual as well as moral existence. Just as, out of the first awakening of a pure human feeling such as Christianity brought us, there rose in contrast to priesthood a work like the "Magic Flute," child-like, artless but devoutly pure and full of feeling, so now there resounds like the mighty watchword of this full national resurrection, Wagner's "Parsifal."

Let us see how the poem itself has done this and what it signifies.

According to the legend of the Holy Grail, already artistically resurrected by the master in "Lohengrin," the chalice from which Christ had drank with His disciples at the last supper, and in which His blood had been received at the cross, had been brought into the western world by a host of angels at a time of most serious danger to the pure gospel of Christianity. King Titurel had erected for it the temple and castle of Monsalvat in the north of Spain, where knights of absolute purity of mind guard it and receive spiritual as well as bodily nourishment from its miraculous powers. This sanctuary can only be found by the pure. The king keeps the holy lance, which had opened the Savior's wound, and with it holds in check the hostile heathen. Klingsor, the sorcerer, on the southern decline of the mountain, rules the latter. He had likewise once been seized with remorse for his sins, his "pain of untamed longings and the most terrible pressure of hellish desires," and had mutilated himself and then seeking deliverance had wandered to the Holy Grail. Amfortas however, Titurel's son, now king of the Grail, perceived his impurity and sternly turned away the evil sorcerer, who only seeks release for worldly gain.

Angered thereat, the latter now contrives through the agency of Kundry, who appears in the highest and most bewitching beauty, encircling the king himself with the snares of passion, to obtain power over him and to wrest from him the lance with which he wounds him. This wound will burn until the holy lance shall be regained. This then is the supreme deed to be accomplished. The Grail itself at one time has proclaimed during the keenest pangs of the suffering king, that it shall be regained by him who, deficient in worldly knowledge, shall from pure sympathy with his terrible sufferings recognize the sufferings of humanity and through such blissful faith bring to it new redemption. The body of humanity, which Christianity had called into new life, had been invaded by a consuming poison and only so far as by the full unconsciousness of innocence, its genius itself was re-awakened, was it possible to again expel the poison.

In the forest of the castle old Gurnemanz and two shield-bearers lie slumbering at early dawn. The solemn morning-call of the Grail is heard and they all rise to pray and then await the sick king who is to take a soothing bath in the near lake. All medicinal herbs have proved useless. Kundry shortly after suddenly appears in savage, strange attire and proffers balm from Arabia. The king is carried forward. We listen to his lamentations. He thanks Kundry, who, however, roughly declines all thanks. The shield-bearers show indignation at this but are reprimanded by Gurnemanz who says: "She serves the Grail and her zeal with which she now helps us and herself at the same time is in atonement for former sins." When she is missing too long, a misfortune surely is in store for the knights. She preserves for them by the opposing forces of her nature the true and good in their consciousness and purpose. With that he tells them Klingsor has established on the other side of the mountain, toward the land of the Arabian infidels, a magic garden with seductively beautiful women to menace them by enticing the knights there and ruining them. In the attempt to destroy this harbor of sin the king had carried away the wound and lost the lance which, according to the revelation of the Grail, only "the simple fool knowing by compassion" could recover.

Suddenly cries of lamentation resound in the sacred forest. A wild swan slowly descends and dies. Shield-bearers bring forward a handsome youth whose harmless, innocent demeanor inspires involuntary interest. He is recognized by the arrows he carries as the murderer of the bird which had been flying over the lake and which had seemed to the king, about to take his bath, as a happy omen. Gurnemanz upbraids him for this deed of cruelty. The swan is doubly sacred to the Grail. It is a swan also that conducts Lohengrin to the relief of innocence! "I did not know," Parsifal replies. The universal lamentation however touches his heart and he breaks his bow and arrows. He knows not whence he came, knows neither father nor name. The only thing he knows is that he had a mother named "Sad-heart." "In forest and wild meadows we were at home." Gurnemanz perceives however by his manner and appearance that he is of noble race, and Kundry, who has seen and heard everything in her constant wanderings confirms the impression.

"Thus he was the born king
Who had the aspect of a lordly youth,"

says Chiron to Faust of the young Herakles. As his father had been slain in battle, the mother had brought him up in the wilderness a stranger to arms—foolish deed—mad woman! Parsifal relates that he had followed "glittering men" and after the manner of the vigorous primitive peoples, had led the wild life of nature, following only natural instincts. Gurnemanz reproaches him for running away from his mother and when Kundry states that she is dead, Parsifal furiously seizes her by the throat. It is the first feeling for a being other than himself, his first sorrow. Again Gurnemanz upbraids him for his renewed violence but remembering the prophecy and the finding of the secret passage to the castle, he believes that there may be nobler qualities in him. For this reason he speaks to him of the Grail, which, now that the king has left the bath, is to provide them anew with nourishment. Upon secret paths they reach the castle of the Grail which only he of pure mind can find. The knights solemnly assemble in a hall with a lofty dome. Beyond Amfortas' couch of pain, the voice of Titurel is heard as from a vaulted niche, admonishing them to uncover the Grail. Thus the dead genii of the world admonish the living to expect life! Amfortas however cries out in grievous agony that he, the most unholy of them all, should perform the holiest act, that in an unsanctified time the sanctuary should be seen. The knights however refer him to the promised deliverance and so begins the solemn unveiling for the distribution of the last love-feast of the Savior, whose cup is then drawn forth, resplendent in fiery purple. Parsifal stands stupefied before this consecration of the human although he also made a violent movement toward his heart when the king gave forth his passionate cry of anguish. But the torments of guilt which produce such sorrows he has not yet comprehended. Gurnemanz therefore angrily ejects him through a narrow side-door of the temple to resume his ways to his wild boyish deeds. He had first to experience the torments of passion and deliverance from the same in his own person.

The second act takes us to Klingsor's magic castle. Klingsor sees the fool advance, joyous and childish, and summons Kundry, the guilty one, who rests in the dead lethargy of destiny, and in sorrow and anger only follows his command. She longs no more for life, but seeks deliverance in the eternal sleep. She has laughed at the bleeding head of John, laughed when she beheld the Savior bleeding at the cross, and is now condemned to laugh forever and to ensnare all in her net of passion: "Whoever can resist thee, will release thee," says Klingsor, the father of evil. "Make thy trial upon the boy." The youth approaches. The fallen knights seek to hinder his progress, but he easily vanquishes them all, and stands victorious upon the battlement of the castle, gazing in childish astonishment at all this unknown silent splendor below. Soon, however, the scene becomes animated. The ravishing enchantresses appear in garments of flowers, and each seeks to win the handsome youth for herself. He remains, however, toward them what he is—a fool. Suddenly he hears a voice. He stands astonished, for he heard the name with which in times long past his mother had called her hearts-blood; it is the one thing he knows. The beauties disappear. The voice takes on form. It is Kundry, no longer of repulsive, savage appearance, but as a "lightly draped woman of superb beauty." She explains to him his name:

"Thee, foolish innocent, I called Fal parsi—
Thee, innocent fool, Parsifal!"

She tells him of his mother's love, of his mother's death. What he, a giddy fool, has thus far done in life, suddenly overwhelms him as well as the thought that despair at his loss has even killed his mother. He sinks deeply wounded at the feet of the seductive woman; it is the first soul-despair in his life. She, however, with diabolic persuasiveness, avails herself of this to overcome his manly heart by her only way, the painful, longing sensation for his mother, and offers him the consolation which love gives, "as a blessing, the mother's last greeting, the first kiss of love." At this he rises quickly in great alarm and presses his hands against his heart. "Amfortas! the wound burns in my heart!" The miracle of knowledge has happened to him, and in a moment has changed his whole nature. It is regeneration by grace, recognized from the earliest time as the sense of all religion. He now experiences the trembling of guilty desires that burn within our breasts, and understands also the mystery of salvation which he can now obtain for the unhappy King of the Grail. Out of the depths of his soul he hears the supplications of the Grail:

"Redeem me, save me
From hands defiled by sin!"

The evil demon of voluptuousness displays all its charms. Astonishment gives way more and more to passion for this pure one, but he sinks into deep and deeper reverie until a second long, burning kiss suddenly and completely awakens him. Then, having gained "world-knowledge," he sees into the deep abyss of this being full of guilt and penitence, and impetuously repulses the temptress. She herself, however, is now overpowered by the passion which she has sought by all the means of temptation to instil into the innocent youth, and fancies she sees in him again the Savior whom she had once laughed at. She tells him with heartrending truth her inextinguishable suffering, her eternal sorrow, her lamentation full of the laughter of derision, the whole wide emptiness of her misery, and implores him to be merciful, and let her weep for a single hour upon his pure bosom—for a single hour to be his. But the answer comes like the voice of an avenging God, terribly stern and annihilating:

"To all eternity thou wouldst be damned with me,
If for one hour I should forget my mission."

At last she seeks, like the serpent in Paradise, to allure him with the promise that in her arms he will attain to godhood. He remains, however, true to himself. Roused now to furious rage, she curses him. He shall never find Amfortas, but shall wander aimlessly. Klingsor then appears, and puts his power to the utmost trial by brandishing his sacred lance, but Parsifal's pure faith banishes the false charm. The lance remains suspended above his head. Kundry sinks down crying aloud. The magic garden is turned to a desert. Parsifal calls out:

"Thou knowest where alone thou canst find me again."

That true womanly love roused for the first time in her will also show this desolate heart the path to eternal love. And Parsifal had finally shown her, the pitiable one, the only thing he could—pity!

The last act takes us once more into the domain of the sacred Grail which Parsifal since then has been longingly seeking. Gurnemanz, now grown to an old man, lives as a hermit near a forest spring. From out the hedges he hears a groan. "So mournful a tone comes not from the beast," he says, familiar as he is with the lamenting sounds of sinful humanity. It is Kundry, whom he carries completely benumbed out of the thicket. This fierce and fearful woman had not been seen nor thought of for a long time. Her wildness now however lies only in the accustomed serpent-like appearance, otherwise she gives forth but that one cry "to serve! to serve!" Whoever has not comprehended the highest and most actual elements of our life when they assert themselves, is condemned to silence. Only by silent acts and conduct can she attest the growing inner participation in the higher and nobler human deeds. She enters the hut close by and busies herself. When she returns with the water pitcher she perceives a knight, clad in sombre armor, who approaches with hesitating steps and drooping head. Gurnemanz greets him kindly but admonishes him to lay aside his weapons in the sacred domain and above all on this the most sacred of days—Good Friday. With that he recognizes him. It is Parsifal, now a mature and serious man. "In paths of error and of suffering have I come," he says. He is at once saluted by Gurnemanz who recognizes the sacred lance as "master" for now he can hope to bring relief to the suffering king of the Grail whose laments Parsifal had once listened to without being moved to action. He learns through the faithful old man of the supreme distress and gradual disappearance of the holy knights. Amfortas has refused to uncover the life-preserving Grail and prefers to die rather than linger in pain and anguish, and thus the strength of the knights has died away. Titurel is already dead, a "man like others," and Gurnemanz has hidden himself in solitude in this corner of the forest. Parsifal is overcome with grief. He, he alone has caused all this. He has for so long a time not perceived the path to final salvation. Kundry now washes his feet "to take from him the dust of his long wanderings," while Gurnemanz refreshes his brow and asks him to accompany him to the Grail which Amfortas is to uncover to-day for the consecration of the dead Titurel. Kundry then anoints his feet and Gurnemanz his head that he may yet to-day be saluted as king and he himself performs his first act as Savior by baptizing Kundry out of the sacred forest spring. Now for the first time can she shed tears. Thereby even the fields and meadows appear as if sprinkled with sacred dew, for according to the ancient legend, nature also celebrates on Good Friday the redemption which mankind gained by Christ's love-sacrifice and which changes the sinner's tears of remorse to tears of joy.

In the castle of the Grail the knights are conducting Titurel's funeral. Amfortas, who in his sufferings longs for death as the one act of mercy, falls into a furious frenzy of despair when the knights urge him to uncover the Grail which alone gives life, so that they all retreat in terror. Then at the last moment Parsifal appears and touches the wound with the lance that alone can close it. He praises the sufferings of Amfortas that have given to him, the timorous fool, "Compassion's supreme strength and purest wisdom's power" and assumes the king's functions. The Grail glows resplendent. Titurel rises in his coffin and bestows blessing from the dome. A white dove descends upon Parsifal's head as he swings the Grail. Kundry with her eyes turned toward him sinks dying to the ground while Amfortas and Gurnemanz do him homage as king and a chorus from above sings:

"Miracle of Supreme blessing,
Redemption to the Redeemer!"

The holy Grail, the symbol of the Savior, has at last been rescued from hands defiled by guilt—has been redeemed.

Such is the short sketch of the grand as well as profoundly significant dramatic action of the artist's last work! It is easy to see that the figures and actions are but a parable. They symbolize the ideas and periods of human development. Nay more, the phases and powers of human nature are here disclosed to view. It is the inner history of the world which ever repeats itself and by which mankind is always rejuvenated. The pure and restored genius of the nation arises anew to its real nature. Its lance heals the wound which we have received at the hands of the other—the evil and foreign genius. It is this pure genius which all, even the dead and the dying, hail as King, and do homage to new deeds of blessing. Next to religion itself, it was art which more than all else constantly brought to the consciousness of humanity the ideals which originated with the former, and here art even entered literally into the service of divine truth. The lance, which signifies the mastery over the spirits, was wrested from the dominating powers. Serious harm indeed and spiritual starvation have followed as the consequence of our falling in every sphere of life under the control of the elements that frivolously play with our supreme ideals. Art, which springs from the purest genius of mankind, seems destined now to be the first to regain the lance and heal the wasting wound. For is not religion divided into warring factions and science into special cliques, jealous of each other? The church does not prevail in the struggle against the evil powers here or elsewhere, and has long ceased to satisfy the mind. The increasing tendency to pursue special studies creates indifference for such supreme ethical questions. It is art alone that has gained new strength from within itself. We have seen it in portraying this one mighty artist, in the irresistible force, in the longing and hoping, in the indestructible, faithful affection for his people, which must dominate all who have retained the feeling for the purely human. Should not art then be destined to awaken, among the cultured at least, a vivid renewal of the consciousness of the sublime for which we are fitted and in whose slumbering embrace we are held? Eternal truth ever selects its own means and ways to reveal itself anew to mankind. "The ways of the Lord are marvelous!" It aims only at the accomplishment of its object. It has at heart only our ever wandering and suffering race. Those who judged without prejudice tell us that this "Parsifal" appeared to them as a mode of divine worship, and that the festival-play-house was not only no longer a theatre, but that even all evil demons had been banished from this edifice, and all good ones summoned within its walls. Would that this were so, and that we could hope in the future that the painful and severe trials of the artist's long life, which gave to this genius also "compassion's supreme strength and purest wisdom's power," would be blessed with abundant fruit, with the full measure of consummation of his own hopes, and the goal so ardently struggled for attained, for his as well as for our own welfare.

However this may be, and whatever the future may have in store for us, this "Parsifal" is a call to the nation grander than any one has uttered before. It was foreordained, and could only be accomplished by an art which is the most unmixed product of that culture originating with Christianity; more, it is a product of the religious emotions of humanity itself. Just as our master said of Beethoven's grand art, that it had rescued the human soul from deep degradation, so no artist after him has presented this supreme and purest spirit of our nation as sanctified and strengthened by Christianity, purer and clearer than he who had already confessed in early years that he could not understand the spirit of music otherwise than as love! With "Parsifal" he has created for us a new period of development, which is to lead us deeper into our own hearts and to a purer humanity, and thereby give us possibly the strength to overcome everything false and foreign which has found its way into our life, and elevate us to a sense of the real object and goal of life.

Richard Wagner, more than any other contemporary, as we conceive, has re-awakened in the sphere of the intellectual life of his German people its inborn feeling for the grand and profound, for the pure and the sublime— in one word, for the ideal. May we who follow prove this in life by gratefully welcoming this grand deed! Then Lohengrin, who sought the wife that believed in him, need not again return to his dreary solitude. He will be forever relieved of his longing for union with the heart of his people. Then too it can be said of him, this genius who throughout a long life "in paths of error and of suffering came" as of all who live their life in love for the whole: "Redemption to the Redeemer."

The biography of Dr. Nohl closes at this point. What remains to be told is shrouded in sadness. It is but a record of suffering and death. In the autumn of 1882, the great master went to Italy, where his fame had already preceded him, and where in the very home of Italian opera his works had been given with great success, to seek rest and improvement of health. He made his home at the Palazzo Vendramin in Venice, where he was joined by Liszt and other friends. With the help of an orchestra and chorus, he was rehearsing some of his earlier works and was also engaged in remodeling his symphony. His restless energy was manifest even in these days of recreation. The *Neue Freie Presse* states that he was composing a new musical drama, called "Die Buesser," based upon a Brahminical legend and having for its motive the doctrine of the transmigration of souls. Filippo Filippi, the Italian critic, also says that he was engaged upon a new opera, with a Grecian subject, in which "it would undoubtedly have been shown that his genius, turning from the misty fables of the Germans to the bright and serene poetry of ancient Greece, would have drawn nearer to our musical life and feeling, which is clear and characteristically melodious." Whatever may have been his tasks it was destined they should not be achieved. "Parsifal" was his swan song. It was during the representation of this opera that his asthmatic trouble grew so intense as to necessitate his departure for Italy and regular medical treatment. During the week preceding his death he was in excellent spirits, and greatly enjoyed the carnival with his family and friends. On the 12th of February he even visited his banker and drew sufficient money to cover the expenses of a projected trip into southern Italy, with his son, Siegfried. On the morning of the 13th he devoted his time as usual to composition and playing. He did not emerge from his room until 2 o'clock when he complained of feeling very fatigued and unwell. At 3 o'clock he went to dinner with the family, but just as they were assembled at table and the soup was being served he suddenly sprang up, cried out "Mir ist sehr schlecht," (I feel very badly) and fell back dead from an attack of heart disease.

The remains were conveyed along the Grand Canal, amid the most impressive pageantry of grief, to the railroad station, and thence transported by a special funeral train to Baireuth. The public obsequies were very simple and impressive, consisting only of the performance of the colossal funeral march from "Siegfried," speeches by friends and a funeral song by the Liederkranz of Baireuth, after which the cortege moved to the tolling of bells to the grave which at his request was prepared behind his favorite villa "Wahnfried," which had been the scene of his great labors. The Lutheran funeral service was pronounced and the body of the great master was laid to its final rest.

The news of his death was received by Angelo Neumann, the director of the Richard Wagner Theatre, on the 14th, at Aachen, just as a performance of the "Rheingold" was about to commence. The director addressed the audience as follows:

"Not only the German people, the German nation, the whole world mourns to-day by the coffin of one of its greatest sons. All in this assembly share our grief and pain. But nevertheless we alone can fully measure the fearful loss which the Richard Wagner Theatre has met with through this event. The love and care of the master for this institution can find no better expression than in a letter, written by his own hand, received by me this evening, which closes with these words:

'May all the blessings of Heaven follow you! My best greetings, which I beg you to distribute according to desert.

'Sincerely yours,
'RICHARD WAGNER.
'VENICE, PALAZZO VENDRAMIN, February 11, 1883.'

"Now we are orphaned—in the Master everything is as if dead for us! I can only add, we shall never cease to labor according to the wishes and the spirit of this great composer; never shall we forget the teachings which we were so happy as to receive from his lips and pen."

A correspondent, writing from Leipzig at the time of his death, contributes some interesting information as to his method of composition and the literary treasures he had left behind him. He says:

"Richard Wagner composed, like all great musicians, in his brain, and not, as is often imagined, at the piano. It is a delight to examine a manuscript composition from his hand—to see how complete and well-rounded, how ripe and finished everything sprung from his head. Changes are very rarely found in such a manuscript; even in the boldest harmonies and most difficult combinations, not a slip of the pen occurs. In the entire score of 'Tannhaeuser,' which Wagner wrote out himself from beginning to end in chemical ink, not one correction is to be found. One note followed the other with easy rapidity. It was his habit to write the musical sketch in pencil—in Baireuth, music-paper was to be found in every corner of 'Wahnfried,' on which while wandering about the house during sleepless nights, musing and planning, he made brief jottings, often merely a new idea in instrumentation. The rest was in his head; the vocal parts were added to the score without hesitation, and never needed correction. For the orchestra he employed three staves, one of which was reserved for special notes, as, for instance, when a particular instrument was to enter. From these sketches the vocal parts could be written out immediately, although the instrumentation was by no means finished. Such sketches were carefully collected by Frau Cosima, who tried for a time to fix the notes permanently by drawing the pen through them. This task was, however, soon abandoned. In its stead she grasped the idea of making a collection of Wagner's manuscripts, to be deposited in 'Wahnfried.' For many years she has conducted an extended correspondence for the purpose of obtaining, for love or money, the scattered treasures, and has, in a great measure— principally through the use of the latter persuasive—succeeded.

"Wagner had written his memoirs, which are not only finished, but already printed. The entire edition consists of *only three copies*, one of which was in the possession of the author, the second an heirloom of Seigfried's, and the third in the hands of Franz Liszt. This autobiography fills four volumes, and was printed at Basel, every proof-sheet being jealously destroyed, so that there are actually but three copies in existence. To the nine volumes of his works already published (Leipzig, E. W. Fritzsch, 1871-'73) will be added a tenth, containing brief essays and sketches of a philosophical character, and (it is to be hoped) the four volumes of the autobiography."

After a life of strife such as few men have to encounter; of hatred more intense and love more devoted than usually falls to the fate of humanity; of restless energy, indomitable courage, passionate devotion to the loftiest standards of art and unquestioning allegiance to the "God that dwelt within his breast," he rests quietly under the trees of Villa "Wahnfried." He lived to see his work accomplished, his mission fulfilled, his victory won and his fame blown about the world despite the malice of enemies and cabals of critics. As the outcome of his stormy life we have music clothed in a new body, animated with a new spirit. He has lifted art out of its vulgarity and grossness. The future will prize him as we to-day prize his great predecessor—Beethoven.

G. P. U.

Buy Books Online from

www.Booksophile.com

Explore our collection of books written in various languages and uncommon topics from different parts of the world, including history, art and culture, poems, autobiography and bibliographies, cooking, action & adventure, world war, fiction, science, and law.

Add to your bookshelf or gift to another lover of books - first editions of some of the most celebrated books ever published. From classic literature to bestsellers, you will find many first editions that were presumed to be out-of-print.

Free shipping globally for orders worth US$ 100.00.

Use code "Shop_10" to avail additional 10% on first order.

Visit today
www.booksophile.com

Lightning Source UK Ltd.
Milton Keynes UK
UKHW040635020323
417918UK00004B/138